THE DEERHOLME
FORAGING BOOK

OLIVER ON THE FORAGING TRAIL

WILD STRAWBERRY

THE
Deerholme
Foraging Book

WILD FOODS AND RECIPES FROM THE PACIFIC NORTHWEST
Bill Jones

TouchWood
Editions

TouchWood Editions
touchwoodeditions.com

LIBRARY AND ARCHIVES CANADA CATALOGUING IN PUBLICATION
Jones, W.A. (William Allen), 1959–, author
The Deerholme foraging book: wild foods and recipes from the Pacific Northwest / Bill Jones.

Includes bibliographical references and index.
Issued in print and electronic formats.
ISBN 978-1-77151-045-5

1. Cooking (Wild foods). 2. Cooking (Marine algae). 3. Cooking
(Shellfish). 4. Wild plants, Edible—Northwest, Pacific—Identification.
5. Edible mushrooms—Identification. 6. Deerholme Farm. 7. Cookbooks.
I. Title.

TX823.J64 2014   641.6   C2013-906206-8

Editor: Cailey Cavallin
Proofreader: Holland Gidney
Design: Pete Kohut
Cover and interior photos by Bill Jones.

We gratefully acknowledge the financial support for our publishing activities
from the Government of Canada through the Canada Book Fund, Canada
Council for the Arts, and the province of British Columbia through the
British Columbia Arts Council and the Book Publishing Tax Credit.

This book is dedicated to my parents, Bill and Joan Jones. For helping me start out in life with both curiosity and the tools to do something about it. I would also like to acknowledge the influence of the great American forager Euell Gibbons. He was an early role model for appreciating the wild pantry and for having way too much fun doing it.

OLIVER WITH MORELS

CONTENTS

A.

B.

C.

INTRODUCTION

It has been about 12,000 years since we emerged from an existence based on hunting and gathering. One could easily image that back then the ability to forage was the most important skill imaginable. Today, it is thought of more as an interesting hobby, or perhaps a way of hedging a bet on an imagined future world apocalypse. Most people I meet seem to love the concept of foraging but are often confused about where to start. Few realize we live in a veritable wonderland of edible delights, with good eating steps away from our doors. Most will agree the idea of free, tasty food and the act of communing with nature strikes a harmonious chord within everyone.

We have obviously evolved from the need for daily foraging for our sustenance. In the modern world, we can easily buy food from a store or order it over the Internet. The ability to forage is not usually needed for day-to-day survival (at least not yet: cue the zombie apocalypse footage). You may, however, find that foraging teaches you important life lessons that serve you well under many circumstances. Ultimately, foraging teaches you how to be resourceful, independent, confident, and humble. Good foraging is also about surviving.

Many people in our society have lost the close connections and rhythms with the seasons we all used to share. Don't get me wrong, I don't look at the past as a utopian time. It may be appealing to think our ancestors looked at our planet the way an infant looks at his mother—with a mixture of wonder, awe, gratitude, and love. It was more like an unrelenting battle to survive against animals, the natural elements, and fellow humans to eke out a meager existence. Living well was making it through a tough winter without starving or freezing. Those who excelled at foraging were appointed the leaders and providers of society.

Here on Vancouver Island, one can easily imagine the local First Nations villages were a beehive of foraging activity. The early settlements on the Pacific coast were built by nomadic foragers. They were probably following their favourite food source over the Bering Strait (then bridged by ice) to settle on the fertile shores and valleys of the coast. Here, food was abundant and rich in nutrients. Large seasonal harvests of berries, shellfish, and salmon could be preserved and stockpiled, allowing time to develop a complex culture. Free time facilitated the development of

A. LARGE PINE MUSHROOM DETAIL B. OREGON GRAPE BERRIES C. ONION SEED HEAD

amazingly intricate artwork and storytelling deep with symbolism and powerfully designed.

In these early settlements, we find a place where a sign of wealth and power was the act of feeding people very well. That is a fact that should cause us to pause in our bipolar world of excess and famine-tinged societies. Many of our modern health problems come down to too much or too little food. Many of the gains of our world come at the expense of our connection to nature and the fundamental rights of all humans. Having enough food to eat should be a priority on our planet. If we had kept the foragers in charge, hunger might now be a historical footnote, a challenge already conquered.

How can foraging help? First of all, foraging is about acquiring and using knowledge. Secondly, it is all about respect. Acquiring this knowledge may empower you to look at your world with a more questioning glance. Who made up the rule that all safe food must be grown using industrial, controlled production? When did we decide that if you pay nothing for an item it is worthless? Why are we obsessed with controlling nature? You may end up seeing the world as more than black and white—it may be tinged with seaweed green and chanterelle yellow.

Foraging teaches us to be resourceful, cautious, frugal, and happy—even just a little bit. In many ways, it is not even the food that is the reward. It is the sense of accomplishment that comes from locating, identifying, and consuming wild food. And like our ancestral super-foragers, we know that people will respect and maybe even love us if we provide them a good meal.

Foraging can be a humbling task; it demands a high price for respect and is often unforgiving with mistakes. Natural hazards and poisonous pitfalls await you with every turn of the path. You need to temper your greed as well—foods that are harvested must be abundant and not at risk of disappearing forever. Harvesting too much food might result in habitat destruction or loss of abundance. Consuming too much wild food at one sitting may result in a revolt from your digestive system, reminding you that moderation is sometimes good for you. Despite all this, the rewards far out way the risks. I hope this book illustrates the joy that can be found in healthy nutritious food: glorious meals can be found at the side of a path—and mushrooms can truly be magical. Many plants improve your health and contain nutrients that can boost your immune system, sharpen brain function, and improve faculties like respiration and digestion.

All of the recipes in this book can be made with wild products you can easily forage. You can also substitute purchased ingredients for all of these foods. Foraged products are sometimes available in the marketplace. Look for establishments that feature local ingredients or visit your local farmers' market. Increasingly, we are seeing foraged foods on menus and gracing the tables at local markets. I also encourage you to grow your own food. It is a simple act that connects us to nature and is deeply satisfying. Go out into the world and see what you can forage; you might be surprised at the abundance and diversity.

Start with the most commonly foraged products, the low-hanging fruit of the foraging world. Build your confidence, then branch out to the more complicated plants, mushrooms, and shellfish. It is a journey into the past that will allow you to commune with the dawn of humanity. Instead of surviving, you might actually find yourself living a little better. The added bonus is that when you are done foraging, you can come home to a warm bath and a relaxing beverage, like a cup of wild mint tea. That's progress I can get behind.

Bill Jones
Deerholme Farm
Cowichan Valley, BC

GRAND FIR TIPS

THE PATHWAY
TO FORAGING

Just to make things clear, this book is not designed to be a field guide to foraging. It is a handbook on the use of wild foods for harvesting, tips for developing a pantry, and recipes for creating wonderful meals. It is not meant to be a definitive guidebook on the subject. There are a lot of great reference books out there (see p. 257) with much more attention to detail and scope. In my research, I personally found that there is almost too much information contained in some of these books. I want to know what stuff tastes good, is harmless, and provides nutrition and benefits to my diet. My goal is to sift through my experiences and present techniques, recipes, and ideas for you to incorporate wild foods into the modern diet.

In our journey into foraging, I will emphasize safety first. It's always best to keep this in mind when entering a world of edible and poisonous substances. Successful foraging is about educating yourself and building up confidence in the identification and preparation of wild products. It is about knowing what to avoid, along with the seasonal variations in plants and shellfish. There are appropriate times for foraging these products, and if you miss that window, then you'll have to wait a full year to get a second chance.

While many wild plants can provide healthy benefits to our diets, quite a few plants do the opposite—they can kill you, place you in a coma, shut down your organs, and cause neurological irregularities. Scared yet? Well good, remember that a healthy respect is key for successful foraging. The best advice is to focus in on a core of tasty and abundant products . . . and leave the rest alone. If you can't leave them alone, perhaps we can work on improving your odds for survival.

Here are my thoughts on where to begin your foraging journey.

FORAGING SURVIVAL SKILLS

New foragers tend to stress out over the potential of eating a poisonous plant or mushroom. In reality, you are far more likely to fall prey to the environment around you. The wilderness is a sometimes inhospitable place. Mossy slopes, downed trees, sinkholes, thorns, and thick brush all lurk quietly, waiting to twist your ankle or break a bone. Most unfortunate incidents would require a call to an ambulance or a visit to an emergency room in the city. In the wilderness, this event can turn into a life-threatening situation far from help. You would benefit from some basic survival knowledge and an awareness of the potential dangers waiting.

Planning

The first rule of thumb is to never venture into the woods alone. It is a rule I sometimes break with my dog as a companion and a cell phone in my pocket. Usually these trips are close to home and in areas I know very well. But keep in mind I have many years of woods and survival experience and an admitted love of danger (my wife says I'm not that bright). Realize that smart phones are urban phones and often have a very limited range in the deep woods. They might be useful for that compass app, but don't count on your phone working when you absolutely need it. I also make it a rule to tell people where I am going and when I expect to return. Solo foraging is not recommended for most people—too much can go wrong, cell calls drop, batteries die, weather changes. In general, if you are going into the deep forest, bring a friend or two and leave a note with your destination, parking location, and time you will return.

Equipment

There are a few things I always bring with me when foraging. Here is my checklist:

- Cell phone
- Pocketknife, good quality (i.e., Swiss Army): I put mine on a cord or lanyard
- Compass: take a reading of the position of your car from the forest's edge
- Backpack, small
- Food (sandwich, fruit, chocolate, granola bar)
- Survival kit (matches, foil blanket, granola bar, bandages, safety pins, etc.)
- Gloves and hat for rain and UV protection, high SPF sunscreen (30+)
- Rain coat: I use Gore-Tex (breathable, water-repellant fabric)
- Optional: wrist watch, camera, GPS
- Bags for collecting products (cloth grocery bags, plastic bags, baskets, etc.)

POTENTIAL HAZARDS

Getting lost

The best foraged materials are often found far from civilization. You might use logging roads or trails as a starting point, but it is easy to get off the grid and into territory that has few or no signs of civilization. A good map is handy to have in the wild; modern technology like a hand-held GPS is also useful for those not familiar with the terrain of the foraging area.

While foraging, there is a tendency to do two dangerous things. One is looking at the ground as you walk. The second is getting carried away by the thrill of the forage. Particularly when you are finding lots of plants or mushrooms, the thrill tends to make you forget things like direction. The natural tendency for most people is to veer off to the left or right when they are walking (even though they may think they are walking in a straight line). Your best low-tech source of direction is often the sun—but this is not helpful if it is cloudy or raining. I like to keep an eye on stream directions and the general layout of hills as I hike. If I am in an area that is not familiar, I tend to work in loops away from a base point (usually my vehicle) and explore the area in expanding circles. Always remember to get out of the woods well before dusk; the light diminishes quickly in the forest.

Natural hazards

Deadfall, rotted stumps, and soft moss are all part of the hazards of foraging. Rotting stumps are particularly treacherous as they can allow your leg to sink suddenly deep into the moss, a potential threat to your bones and knee ligaments. High winds are another dangerous hazard in the woods: tree branches break off, trees uproot, and dead trees can become dangerous projectiles. Leave the woods quickly if high winds occur.

Foraging on the seashore has its own set of complications. The forage zones around rocks are slippery and it can be easy to trip and fall in the water. There are dangerous currents called rip tides that can quickly whisk you out to sea, sometimes with undertow currents that drag you down. Be very careful around rocks and seaside cliffs. Erosion is always at work on these cliffs, making their edges very fragile and prone to collapse.

The beach is also bombarded with UV rays, which makes getting a sunburn a very real possibility. Combine this with a windburn and you could be in for a few painful days. I always add a good hat and sunscreen to the list of foraging tools for the seashore. And don't forget your lips—the wind and sun will dry them out quickly and result in chapped and cracked lips. I carry lip balm in my backpack to protect mine.

Wildlife

It is fairly common to come across animals like bears while foraging in the forest. Happily, bears will usually run away and leave you alone. Most bears are doing the same thing you are: foraging for berries. They have poor eyesight, so they will hear and smell you before they see you. You should be concerned if you see a freshly killed carcass, or small bear cubs nearby. Slowly back away from these bears and head off in the opposite direction. If you are placed in a bad position (i.e., being attacked), you can try using bear spray (hot pepper spray) or hitting the bear sharply on the nose or in the eyes—repeatedly. This is easier said than done. A brown bear can weigh up to 1,500 pounds (680 kg) and has very strong teeth and claws. The bear will often try to attack your head and neck, so the best advice is to curl up in a ball and wrap your hands around your neck. Actually, the very best advice is to avoid a confrontation—it is far less painful. Most bears are just as scared of you. However, bears that wander through towns or garbage dumps are more dangerous, as they have been conditioned to not fear humans.

Cougars are another threat here in the Pacific Northwest. Although naturally shy, cougars are sometimes attracted to dogs and small children. They hunt around dusk, so it is never a good idea to be foraging at this time of the day. Cougar attacks are more common if the natural food of the cougar is scarce (deer, rabbits, etc.) or the animal is in distress and desperate. Most serious animal attacks in our region involve cougars.

My beach travels have resulted in several encounters with wolves. They are often chasing other prey or just hanging out at the beach with the rest of us. Wolves are naturally shy and tend to stay away from humans and civilizations. They are usually far more interested in the local deer population; if you see a carcass, move away as quickly as possible.

Ticks are another common pest of Pacific Northwest forests. Be sure to remove any ticks as soon as possible. The tick is a mild irritant but they do occasionally harbour bacteria that can result in Lyme disease. This is a serious infection that has debilitating effects; the classic symptoms are a circular expanding rash around the bite, followed by severe and persistent flu like systems (sometimes lasting months). The best protection against ticks is covering your skin with clothing, tucking pants into your socks, and wearing a hat. They are fairly rare, but ticks may have serious consequences.

Poisonous plants

There are many poisonous plants and mushrooms lurking out in the wild. I have tried to focus on the safer bets for foraging, but every aspect of gathering wild plants has some risks. One of the nastiest plants out there is commonly known as water hemlock (*Cicuta* species, locally *Cicuta douglasii*). It contains a toxin (cicutoxin) that has a damaging effect on the central nervous system, leading to convulsions, loss of

Pacific Northwest Resources for Poisoning Help

British Columbia Drug and Poison Information Centre (dpic.org)
    Hotline: 1-800-567-8911
Canadian Association of Poison Control Centres (capcc.ca)
Oregon Poison Center (ohsu.edu/poison)
    Hotline: 1-800-222-1222
Washington Poison Center (wapc.org)
    Hotline: 1-800-222-1222

consciousness, and death in some cases. To make matters worse, these plants are easily mistaken for common edible plants like wild celery, cow parsnip, and wild carrots.

Many other plants contain compounds (toxins, acids, psychoactive compounds) that are potentially detrimental to your health and well-being. Positive identification is a critical first step to keeping safe. Always make sure you are identifying the plant correctly before ingesting any wild product. Even then, some people's metabolism or general health levels will not tolerate some wild plants. People with compromised immune systems and kidney or liver issues should be particularly careful with their usage of wild plants.

In most regions, there are Poison Control response centres that are manned by specialists in poisonous substances. They are experts in identifying poisons and can create a life-saving plan of action for those affected. If you have an issue with something you have eaten, it is handy to have a sample or photo to aid in identification. Inducing vomiting is usually the first line of defense, along with ingesting fluids to flush the toxins through the liver and kidneys. Get help immediately.

Shellfish Poisoning

There is a dizzying array of common shellfish illnesses associated with contaminated products. These include bacteria and symptom types like *Vibrio parahaemolyticus*, hepatitis A, norovirus, Paralytic Shellfish Poisoning (PSP), amnesic shellfish poisoning (ASP), and diarrhetic shellfish poisoning (DSP). Symptoms may appear within a few hours or may take a number of days to develop. These dangers are the reason it is critical never to harvest near populated areas or where harvest bans are in place.

Paralytic Shellfish Poisoning (PSP)

The most serious danger from consuming shellfish comes from PSP. The worst-case scenario is death; this should always get your attention. When conditions are right (usually in warmer weather) large, naturally occurring algal blooms appear in ocean waters. Occasionally (but not always) these reach proportions high enough that the waters appear reddish. The algae produce toxins (saxitoxin is one of the most prevalent) that can impair the respiratory system and lead to coma and death in the worst cases. The toxin is prevalent in filter-feeding shellfish like clams, mussels, oysters, and scallops. Commercially harvested shellfish are tested for this toxin and when PSP is detected in local waters, shellfish harvesting is suspended.

The signs of poisoning are numbness in the mouth, lips, arms, and face. In more serious cases, sufferers exhibit loss of coordination, respiratory problems, coma, and occasionally death.

It is also important to always cook products thoroughly to kill some (but not all) of these toxins.

HARVESTING THE WILD

As a forager, you are forced to make a series of judgment calls on the suitability of the foraged materials. Is the environment free of contamination? Is the plant ready for harvesting? Is the plant past its prime? Am I absolutely sure of the identification? These judgments in the field are crucial to finding safe products and to ensuring you make the best of a precious resource.

Seeking a healthy environment

The environment surrounds us: land, water, and air. It is often an incredibly nurturing cradle of fertility; occasionally, it is harsh and unforgiving. Taking a health survey of the harvest environment is a critical step. Are there signs of civilization nearby—roadways, buildings, signs of pollution? Pollution can take on many disguises, from an oily sheen on the water (a sign of contamination) to the aroma of industrial fluids, or the presence of garbage and abandoned equipment or vehicles. Many people choose the strangest and most beautiful places to dump their refuse. Wild plants

A.

B.

C.

D.

readily suck up contaminants in their growth. In this way, they are indicators of environmental health. Plants may look healthy and may indeed thrive in conditions that create dangerous compounds. Urban areas in particular are sources of nasty chemicals and rich sources of bacterial contamination. Mushrooms in particular may be compromised with heavy metals, radiation, and dangerous chemicals. These are man-made interactions and the presence of nearby signs of civilization and wild foods living together should always give you pause for concern. This factor makes foraging in urban areas relatively risky. It may be possible to harvest healthy and clean food in these environments but the odds of finding compromised food increases with the level of human activity around the plants. So where do you go? As far away as possible from civilization might be the best advice.

Seasons and variation

The timing of foraged product depends on many factors. Along the Pacific coast, the seasons arrive at different times, depending on a few factors. Latitude dictates the amount of sunlight and darkness each day receives. Altitude of the location affects the daily temperatures, and orientation (north, south, east, west) plays a role in when plants emerge and grow to maturity.

In general, plants growing in areas with lower altitude and good exposure to sunlight will mature sooner. Areas like north-facing slopes at higher elevations may be a month or more behind. Mushrooms rely on a combination of moisture and sunlight to fruit; they may need a blend of these conditions to make the right mixture for abundant harvesting.

These reasons are why the best foragers take years to know the climate and terrain of a region. They may need to go to different areas each year to obtain the correct combination of conditions. This is as much art as it is science. Careful observation is the best teacher.

In our region, look to the spring for the best greens and shoots from trees and berries. The first mushroom harvest starts with morels and oyster mushrooms. Summer is primetime for berries, with the first chanterelles and lobster mushrooms also appearing. Fall is all about tree fruits and the vast majority of the mushroom harvest.

A. PINE SHOOTS B. BLACKBERRIES C. CATTAIL D. YELLOW CHANTERELLES

Finally, the winter months are peak seasons for shellfish and a special treat—tapping the bigleaf maples to create wondrous syrup. There are amazing products to be found in all our seasons.

Natural selection

Wild foods are out there at the mercy of the elements, animals, and insects. The plants that are edible to us are usually edible to a host of creatures. Many wild greens are best in the spring when they are young, tender, sweeter, and less prone to insect damage and infestation. Pick specimens that have whole leaves and do not appear wilted, damaged, or diseased.

Berries are best when they have ripened fully. The berry is often sour and bitter up until that point. While there are some uses for these sour and bitter components, most of us will want the berries when they are sweet and succulent. Unfortunately, this is the time many other creatures also want the sweet fruit. Bears, mice, deer, birds, squirrels—the list could go on and on. Pick berries when they are firm, sweet, and plump. Don't forget to leave a few behind for the wildlife!

Moulds are a particular concern for wild food and mushroom foraging. Parasitic moulds attack certain mushrooms often with an increased risk for allergy issues and stomach upsets. Berries and foods with higher sugar contents are subject to wild yeast and may even ferment while on the plant. Wrinkled, discoloured, and mouldy foods should be separated and discarded.

Mushroom harvesting tips

Mushrooms are a perishable product that begins to deteriorate as soon as you pick it. The more delicate the mushroom, the faster this deterioration will occur. One of your first considerations should be conservation. Mushrooms are the fruit of a much bigger organism whose main job it is to produce spores to help the plant reproduce. I usually forage for mushrooms that are relatively plentiful (like the ones I have described in this book [see pp. 49–61]).

If you find a large patch of mushrooms, resist the urge to pick every specimen. For one thing, there will usually be a wide range of quality in the mushrooms. Young buttons may look great but they will not have had time to develop a depth of flavour.

Older mushrooms will be starting to decay and perhaps be riddled with worm larva. I tend to high-grade mushrooms in the field and take only the best, making sure to leave any questionable mushrooms behind.

If you include wormy mushrooms in your harvest, beware as the larva will migrate to the other, untouched mushrooms as they sit in transport or storage. This is particularly important to watch for with porcini and pine mushrooms.

There is much debate over the correct way to harvest mushrooms. In a mossy forest floor habitat, I feel it is best to gently push the mushroom until it detaches from the mycelium (underground mushroom body) and then pull it up from the forest floor. At that point, you can trim any dirt from the base and clean off as much debris as possible. I never allow dirt to enter my collecting basket or bag. I have no real preference between using baskets or cloth, or even plastic, bags—as long as I immediately place the mushrooms in a packing basket when I return to my vehicle. If you store the mushrooms in a plastic bag for any length of time, they will sweat moisture and the decay process will be accelerated.

Other mushrooms occur on the trunks and stumps of trees (like the oyster mushroom and the cauliflower fungus). These mushrooms must be cut off with a knife as they are harvested. Oyster mushrooms are fragile, so I prefer to use a basket for collecting delicate specimens. A bag would jostle and crush these mushrooms.

In general, try to keep mushroom types separate. Don't worry too much about similar cousins like hedgehogs, chanterelles, etc. These you can sort out back at the house. If there are fragile mushrooms, you can place them in a paper bag and keep then apart in your collecting basket. If you are unsure about the ID of a mushroom, it is a good idea to keep the mushroom separate until it can be identified with certainty (using a guidebook or other expert opinion).

Quality control

Back in the kitchen, I like to soak greens in a big pan of cold water and remove any dirt, dust, and foreign materials from the harvest. I keep all the different plants separate and process them quickly if needed (i.e., stinging nettles). Or I spin them dry in a salad spinner and place them in a small container covered with a damp cloth. Most greens will keep fresh for a couple of days this way.

Depending on the type of berry, berries must usually be handled delicately. You can give them a quick rinse but avoid soaking the berries as it may speed up their decay. Remove any leaves and foreign materials as well as any unripe or damaged fruit. It is wise to process the berries quickly as some are prone to breaking down or developing moulds quickly.

After a mushroom harvest, lay out newspapers on a table and spread out your collection. Go through the mushrooms to confirm the identification, discarding any that you are unsure of. You also have a second opportunity to clean the mushrooms, trimming off any brown edges of the mushrooms. It is important to check for worms (and worm trails) and discard any specimens that are riddled with worms. Failing to do so will result in the transfer of the worms to all the adjacent mushrooms. Make sure to brush off any debris and to wipe the mushrooms with a wet cloth if they appear soiled. If the mushrooms are very wet (like chanterelles tend to be) you can leave the mushrooms out for several hours. Moisture will evaporate and be absorbed by the newspapers. Choose a storage container with plenty of side ventilation (see p. 18) and line it with paper towels or newspaper. Place the cleaned mushrooms inside and top with more paper. Here you need a judgment on the moisture content of the mushrooms. If they appear dry, sprinkle a little water on the top to keep the mushrooms hydrated. If the mushrooms appear wet, do not add any additional water, just place in the refrigerator overnight.

Whatever your harvest, it is a good idea to make plans to process (dry, preserve, etc.) the products within a few days. Like any fresh product, they start to deteriorate the moment they are picked. The more delicate and fragile the material, the greater the urgency to deal with the harvest before it begins to deteriorate.

BUILDING A WILD FOODS PANTRY

There are many excellent techniques that you can use to preserve foraged products so that you can continue to enjoy them months after the original harvest. All of the specific products mentioned in this chapter are covered in detail in the chapter entitled "A Wild Foods Primer" (p. 25).

DAYLILY BUDS

PINE MUSHROOM BUTTONS

DRYING

Dehydrating is one of the best techniques for preserving wild foods. Removing water extends the shelf life of many products like mushrooms and berries. Greens are best consumed fresh but dehydration can be used to make teas and seasoning mixtures. Seaweed can be dehydrated to make excellent products with a long shelf life. I use a high-end home unit made by Excalibur. It is basically a box with twelve racks that can be loaded up with fruit, vegetables, or mushrooms and set to gently dry products over a number of hours or overnight. If you process a lot of food, it is highly recommended. The drying takes place by the use of a fan and a small thermostat-controlled heat source. The gentle and continuous air dries the product evenly without browning the product. It makes prefect dried berries and tasty fruit leathers from purées, and is a great way to almost infinitely preserve a harvest of wild mushrooms. Alternative methods are sun drying on racks, using an oven on the lowest setting (with the door cracked open), or placing the materials on a rack over a heat source like a water heater, wood stove, or heating radiator.

Once I have dehydrated a product, I use a vacuum sealer to keep the product crisp and keep moisture out of the product. Unsealed products will gradually reabsorb moisture, particularly in moist environments or seasons. Properly sealed the materials will have a very long shelf life, possibly for several years if kept in a dark and cool place.

POWDERS

Mushroom powder

Dried mushrooms pack a lot of flavour. Grinding the dried mushroom into a powder allows you to take those flavours to a whole new world of cooking. I use the powder to infuse mushroom flavour in many of my recipes. The key to grinding the mushroom into a powder is starting with a very dry mushroom. A dried mushroom will tend to reabsorb moisture out of the atmosphere it is stored in. If the mushroom is soft and bendable, reheat it in an oven heated to 350°F (180°C) for 2 to 3 minutes. Allow the mushroom to cool (it will crisp up as it cools). Use a small electric coffee grinder (or spice grinder) to make small batches of powder. The powder will keep indefinitely if stored in a tightly closed container. Porcini is my favourite mushroom to grind, but shiitake, button, and fairy ring mushrooms also make great powders.

Seaweed powder

Much like mushrooms, dried seaweed can be used to infuse a lot of flavour into baked goods, sauces, and even protein drinks. The seaweed will add a little salt to whatever you are making so keep this in mind when using the powder. The easiest seaweed to make powders from is the *Porphyra* (nori) family. It is a delicate seaweed that dries well and easily crumbles into a powder.

Grind seaweed in a spice grinder and store in a glass container with a tight-fitting lid. I use canning jars. Will store indefinitely if kept dry.

FREEZING

Freezing is another excellent modern way to store the wild harvest for an extended time. For products like stinging nettles, I soak the leaves in cold water, blanch them in boiling salted water, then drain and refresh in cold water. After squeezing out the excess water, you can freeze the nettles in zip-lock bags for up to 2 months. Placing the nettles in a vacuum bag will extend their life and quality even further. This can be repeated with many wild greens. Vacuum packing products before freezing will increase the shelf life, reducing the chance of freezer burn and the absorption of off odours from other contents of the freezer.

Firm mushrooms can be frozen as is, just place on a tray or in a bag and freeze. Once they thaw, the mushrooms will release a lot of juice. A great trick is to cook the mushroom while partially frozen (just thawed enough to cut with a chef knife). Some mushrooms like chanterelles or more delicate mushrooms like oysters are best when sautéed in oil or butter before freezing. The fat will help to coat the mushroom and preserve the aromatic flavours once thawed. Chanterelles in particular tend to oxidize and become bitter when frozen. Using lots of fat to cook the mushrooms will coat the product and minimize the contact with oxygen.

Berries benefit from freezing initially on a tray, allowing you to break up the berries into individual lumps for easier use straight from the freezer. You can also put the berries directly into freezer bags. The downside is the berries may stick together in a large lump if there is any quantity of juice or crushed berries in the mix. This is more of an issue with softer berries like the blackberry.

Shellfish can be frozen in water with 1 teaspoon (5 mL) of salt added per cup.

Shuck product, place in a zip-lock bag, and cover with salted water. It will keep frozen for 1 to 2 months. Seaweed can also be frozen using this salted water technique.

PRESERVING AND CANNING

At one point, preserving held a prominent place in every kitchen pantry. That was before the freezer became a staple of every modern household. Preserving still is a wonderful technique to use for foraged foods if you use high-sugar or high-acid techniques for preserving. There are important rules to follow when canning foods. The process can create an anaerobic environment, which essentially means "without the presence of large amounts of oxygen." It's a prime environment for nasty spores like botulism to flourish. The anaerobic process is not all bad. It is also responsible for fermentation, which gives us wonderful products like dill pickles and kim chee. These products usually rely on salt (sometimes with the help of chilies) to moderate the levels of harmful bacteria.

Unfortunately, there are well-documented cases of mass poisoning from home-canned mushrooms (particularly in oil and when garlic is present—as it is a natural carrier of botulism spores). This can result in serious illness and even death in extreme cases. Pickling with salt, vinegar, and sugar, however, is a relatively safe method of preservation. This is a complicated subject so please consult a good, modern canning resource (like bernardin.ca or freshpreserving.com) for more details. The pickle recipes in this book are made to be consumed quickly and stored in the refrigerator. This eliminates many of the issues with pickling. (See pp. 86 and 88 for recipes.)

In my jam recipe (p. 78), I choose to use pectin to help set the jam. Pectin is a naturally occurring substance that contributes to jelling. It helps to somewhat lower the sugar volume needed to set the fruit and is a soluble dietary fibre. As a bonus, some newer research has suggested that pectin helps to lower cholesterol levels.

Before you begin the canning process, rinse your jars and place them in a boiling water canner. Cover them with water and bring the water to a boil. Add the jar lids and simmer for at least 5 minutes. Keep simmering while you make your jam or preserves.

INFUSIONS

An infusion is the steeping of a substance in liquid (or oil) to extract therapeutic or culinary properties. We have been doing this since the dawn of civilization with soups,

teas, and elixirs. You can use water, alcohol, or oils and fat (olive oil, butter, duck fat, etc.) to extract many of these flavour and medicinal components.

The safest infusions are made with vinegar or alcohol (both are natural preservatives). A re-emerging hot trend is to create infusions with alcohol to flavour cocktails. The Japanese have been infusing sake with pine mushrooms for many years. The process is fairly simple. Here are a few delicious examples:

Grand Fir Vodka

Grand fir needles add a great flavour to the alcohol. You can also use rum or gin with excellent results. Other needles like spruce and pine work well. You could also use rose petals or aromatic herbs like wild fennel to infuse the liquid.

1 cup (250 mL) grand fir tips, needles only

1 bottle (26 oz [800 mL]) good-quality vodka

Place the grand fir needles in a clean 1-quart (1 L) mason jar. Top up with the vodka and screw on the top. Set on your counter for 1 week. The mixture can be strained or you can keep the whole batch in the refrigerator.

Wild Berry Rumtopf

A rumtopf is a traditional German drink made with seasonal fruit, sugar, and rum. You can use any combination of wild berries to make this concoction. You can sometimes find ceramic jars used for this purpose in antique stores—they are very similar to crock pots used to ferment sauerkraut. The rumtopf was often made in the late summer and kept on the countertop to infuse until Christmas.

4 cups (1 L) mixed wild berries (blackberries, blueberries, salal berry, etc.)

2 cups (500 mL) sugar

3 cups (750 mL) white rum

Quickly rinse the berries and place in a large ceramic or glass jar with a lid. Add the sugar and toss to mix. Cover the berries with the rum (add a little water if needed to cover the berries). Place a piece of plastic over the jar mouth and cover with the lid. Place on the counter and let infuse for at least 1 month.

If the mixture bubbles and appears to be fermenting, add more rum to stop the

A. GRAND FIR TIPS B. DRYING PORCINI MUSHROOMS

fermenting process. For an enhanced forest flavour, you can also add fir, spruce, or pine needles to the infusion for an interesting and delicious effect.

Rosehip Vinegar

Harvest rosehips after the weather turns cool and the trees have dropped their leaves. A light frost is good for creating a little sweetness in the rosehips.

2 cups (500 mL) rosehips (trimmed of stems)

2 cups (500 mL) cider vinegar

1 Tbsp (15 mL) honey

Rinse the rosehips and cut in half, add to a 4-cup (1 L) glass canning jar. Cover with the vinegar and add the honey. Stir to dissolve honey. Place on counter to steep for 1 week. Transfer to refrigerator and let sit for at least 3 more weeks. Strain into a glass container and use as a salad dressing and cooking ingredient. Keeps in refrigerator indefinitely.

SALT

It is surprisingly easy to make your own sea salt. Take 10 quarts (10 L) of seawater and boil it down until the salt crystalizes. You can skim the layer of salt crystals that form on top to make your own fleur de sel (literally "salt flowers"—tiny crystals of salt). You will find it takes a lot of time and energy to create the salt, although it is highly satisfying.

Salt has been used as a preservative since the dawn of civilization. It creates an environment that is inhospitable to bacteria. Salt can also be used to preserve delicate flavours like truffles or aromatic herbs. I process salt and wild herbs to create unusual flavours and beautiful colouring.

Grand Fir Salt

Also works with spruce and pine needles. This technique can also be used to create flavoured salts with dehydrated berries (such as salal or red huckleberry).

2 cups (500 mL) sea salt

1 cup (250 mL) grand fir needle tips

Preheat oven to 200°F (95°C). In a food processor, add salt and needle tips. Pulse until a fine green powder is obtained. Transfer to a warm oven and heat for 20 minutes or until salt feels dry. Allow to cool, and then transfer to a glass jar with a tight-fitting lid. Salt will keep indefinitely.

A WILD FOODS PRIMER

The following is a brief overview of many of the wonderful, delicious wild foods that can be foraged here in the Pacific Northwest. From berries, greens, and mushrooms to seaweed, shellfish, and crustaceans, there are so many products that you can discover. You can start in your own backyard but the best products will be found on a trip to the wild areas of our region.

BLACKBERRY FLOWER

FORESTS AND FIELDS

1) Berries

Berries literally are the low-hanging fruit. Start here and you will immediately feel like a master forager. If you live in the Pacific Northwest, chances are you have picked berries at some point. They are a truly abundant product of our fields, forests, and shores. Whether you were a child with berry juice smearing your face, happily plucking them off the bushes, or an adult filling an ice cream bucket with delicious nuggets, most of us have already experienced the delicious world of foraging. You can think of this as a gateway to the wonderful world of edible wild plants.

Berries are everywhere. They are part of the reproductive process of plants and an important food for our wildlife. Blackberries are sometimes so abundant they press against the edges of civilization, weaving through abandoned cars and twisting through the fences, straining to expand and capture more sunlight and nutrients. You get the feeling if we were to let down our guard, blackberries would eventually take over everything we have carved out in civilization.

One of the best producers of fruit is Himalayan Blackberry. It actually sprung from the soils of Armenia and Iran. This robust plant has aggressively expanded to many corners of the planet and produces copious amounts of sweet berries. It was introduced to North America about 130 years ago and now dominates the landscape of the Pacific Northwest. Like many other foraged plants, it is an invasive species with benefits. If you can't find the Himalayan Blackberry, you are probably not trying.

You tend to notice the blackberries first with their voracious growth, sweet berries, and large thorns, but if you look closely you will also find huckleberries, blueberries, wild strawberries, and many other wonderful finds. On my farm, I can't walk 10 feet without coming across three or four types of edible berries. They are nature's alluring bait, built to entice animals and birds to eat them and transport the seeds to new locations. This is one reason berries travel far and wide.

There are poisonous berries throughout the region. Many are bitter or strangely coloured (pure white for example). Correct identification is important for any wild foods you are going to consume. But you could easily stick with the basic blackberries, blueberries, huckleberries, and salal berries and have excellent success foraging.

Blackberry (*Rubus* spp.) There are almost 400 species of blackberry that appear all over the planet. Our Pacific Northwest native variety is the trailing blackberry (*R. ursinus*). The plant favours the edges of forests and paths and fruits the earliest of the blackberries. The fruit is tiny, sweet, and very aromatic. It is perhaps the tastiest of the blackberries but takes a lot of work to pick any quantity. Look for the trailing berry on the ground, sometimes in large masses near the edge of forests. The leaves are small and pointed with a wrinkled appearance in the centre (along vein lines) and a fine-toothed edge.

The Himalayan Blackberry (*R. armeniacus*) is an aggressive, introduced species that readily adapts to all kinds of urban and rural environments. The plant grows in dense patches and tends to fruit berries in the thousands. The plant will also use nearby trees to gain access to sunlight and nutrients. The Himalayan Blackberry fruits in late July and sometimes continues fruiting into the late fall. It is distinguished by its impressive mass (canes can grow up to 30-feet [9 m] long) and oval leaves with a toothed edge.

The third major type of blackberry is the Cutleaf Evergreen Blackberry (*R. laciniatus*). This is an escapee from commercial cultivation and creates berries that fruit a little later in the year (late summer to fall). It is distinguished by its deeply cut leaves and dense fruit. It is a much smaller plant than the Himalayan Blackberry and tends to grow in circular clumps. The skins are a little firmer than the Himalayan berries and produce a fine and delicate flavour.

Blueberry (*Vaccinium* spp.) Having grown up in Nova Scotia, I have special ties to blueberry picking. Luckily, the Pacific Northwest is also an abundant habitat for these berries. It is possible to pick buckets full of wild blueberries, which have a superior flavour over the larger commercial varieties. There are several closely related species of blueberries and huckleberries that often grow under the same conditions. You could easily mix up the different species on the same foraging expedition. It doesn't really matter; they are all delicious and choice fruits. Blueberries are high in antioxidants and make great desserts, jellies, jams, vinegars, wines, and infusions.

Blueberries freeze very well and take little effort to clean and process. No wonder they are a favourite fruit of both bears and humans. A common coastal variety, *V. ovalifolium*, has smooth oval-shaped leaves, white flowers, and grows in bushes up to 5-feet (1.5 m) tall.

RASPBERRY

Oregon Grape (*Mahonia repens* or *M. aquifolium*) These beautiful green plants resemble holly and have a sharp, wavy edge that can scrape and cut flesh if you brush by it. There are at least two species that appear in our region, one is a low-level bush (*M. repens*) and the other (*M. aquifolium*) is a taller bush that reaches 3 feet (1 m) in size.

The leaves often blush reddish around the edges in late fall. In the spring, a yellow flower cluster emerges that is edible with a nice citric acidity. The green berries are good when pickled or made into forest capers. In fall, the berry clusters redden and eventually turn a deep purple with a whitish frosting on the surface. If left on the plant, the berries will shrivel like raisins.

The berries make an excellent jelly if harvested before the first frost. They have an excellent proportion of pectin. After a frost, they are sweeter but the pectin levels are reduced; I make these berries into syrup or infuse them in cider vinegar. The Oregon grape is considered to contain very high levels of phytonutrients (such as antioxidants) and is an excellent source of vitamin C.

Red Huckleberry (*Vaccinium parvifolium*) This plant is a beautiful ornamental as well as a provider of delicious berries. The red huckleberry is distinguished by its small teardrop leaves and elegant structure, kind of like a natural form of bonsai. The shrub is very common and in good years is loaded with so many berries that the branches dip toward the ground.

The taste is tart and sweet, similar to a red currant. The berries freeze very well and are excellent for pancakes, baking, and sauces. The red huckleberry ripens mid-summer to fall, depending on elevation and southern exposure.

Salal Berry (*Gaultheria shallon*) Salal leaves are a major cash crop in the Pacific Northwest. Their main use is as a florist green. The leaves are oval and thick with a waxy appearance to the surface. The berries are also a prime food source for bears and other animals. Salal berries ripen in the fall and have a dry somewhat mealy texture but fine huckleberry-like flavour. The berries contain high levels of pectin and make a truly excellent jam or jelly. I also use the pulp to infuse vinegar and alcohol.

Salal was a widely distributed and abundant berry on the coast and very important to First Nations. The berries were eaten fresh or dried into cakes for use in the winter months. The cakes were dipped in eulachon grease (from a small ocean smelt, processed for its rich oil). Making the cakes was quite a process. One method was to drop hot rocks into cedar boxes to reduce the berries into paste. The paste was dried in rectangular boxes lined with skunk cabbage leaves and sometimes smoked over an alder fire. This produced an aromatic and nutrient-dense cake.

The plant is dominant in the undergrowth edges of forests. Areas above some beaches are so thick with salal they are almost impenetrable.

Salmonberry (*Rubus spectabilis*) These berries were named for their resemblance to salmon eggs and they often grow alongside streams and areas with available moisture. The berry slips easily from the base and in this way is similar to a raspberry. There are a few colour variations in the berries, some are salmon orange with a red tinge and other berries ripen to a deep red colour. The berry is moderately sweet and highly perishable. They are best eaten as a treat on the trail or mixed with other berries.

The salmonberry is one of the earlier ripening berries, sometimes as early as late June. The flower is a beautiful pink and lilac blossom, good in salads but often filled with tiny insects. (To get rid of bugs, soak the blossoms in cold, salted water before draining and using.) The leaves appear in groups of three, with the leading edge slightly larger than the two side leaves. They have a toothed edge and soft texture.

Local First Nations groups ate the new sprouts in spring and the berries in early summer. The sprouts (or new shoots) were peeled and eaten with salmon or eulachon grease. The berries were eaten fresh as they are too watery to dry with any success.

Thimbleberry (*Rubus parviflorus*) The thimbleberry plant is characterized by large maple-like leaves and smooth, thorn-less branches. The leaves have a fine-toothed edge and are softly fuzzy. It is a common plant of the region, often growing next to salmonberry and blackberry bushes. The berry is a shallow fruit, very similar in appearance to a raspberry. Ripe fruit takes on a reddish or almost black tone. These berries are a little dry but the flavour is excellent. I often use them to infuse vinegar.

The First Nations used the berry extensively for drying, often mixing them with salal berries. On the west coast of Vancouver Island, they made a special cake with

A. SALAL BERRIES B. BLUEBERRIES C. SALMONBERRY

A.

B.

C.

thimbleberries and dried clams. The cakes were flattened and sundried. The new sprouts were also peeled and eaten with eulachon grease.

Wild Strawberry (*Fragaria* spp.) Strawberry is common as a ground cover at the edge of pathways and fields. The berries fruit in late summer and are very tiny. The berries are so small it takes herculean effort to pick any quantity. I usually just use them for a tiny flavour burst while on hiking trails. In addition to these tasty small berries, the leaves of the plant are rich in vitamin C and make a good tea, fresh or dried. The medicinal uses are mainly tea used for urinary tract infections, promoting heart health, and boosting the immune system.

2) Recommended Edible Wild Greens and Plants

Many of the greens, berries, and herbs we hunt for the table are not native to the Pacific Northwest. They spread with the migration of people and were helped along in many cases by animals and birds. Dandelions, lamb's quarters, sorrel, and many others were cultivated as herbs or soup ingredients (potage) and encouraged to grow beyond the confines of the garden. And grow they did. Many of the plants are now considered invasive species that reduce the value of other commercial field crops, such as hay. Corporations have spent billions developing herbicides and genetically engineering crops to lessen the impact of the cursed "weeds." It is ironic that many of the weeds are more nutritious than the crops we try to protect. They are also available for free. I would imagine this greatly irritates those who massage the corporations' profit calculations.

There are many poisonous plants out there. The correct identification of plants is therefore critical. Many plants have poisonous look-alikes that can easily confuse people. Only eat what you are 100 percent sure of.

I only pick plants that are abundant. Many plants are found in specific ecosystems; sometimes they are very sensitive and can even be endangered by disturbing and harvesting the plants. I try to avoid these plants, even if they have a long history of use in the region.

Important examples of plants to avoid are regional flower bulbs. Many plants like camas or forest lily bulbs were once commonly eaten as delicacies by local First Nations.

A. RED HUCKLEBERRIES B. THIMBLEBERRY C. ROSEHIPS

These plants exist in the wild today, but traditionally they were harvested in meadows and often tended in "forest gardens" to encourage the production of plant material. Several of these commodities were treated as money or served to very special guests as a sign of the highest respect. Many of the techniques for increasing production have been lost or discouraged (like burning meadows to promote growth). In many cases, habitat destruction has limited, and in some instances jeopardized, the continued harvest of these plants. For this reason, I made a conscious effort here not to focus on too many wild plants that have edible tubers and roots. The potential environmental damage does not justify the reward. One notable exception is the taproot of the burdock plant. Burdock is an abundant (some would say too abundant) invasive species and happens to be very delicious.

Broadleaf Dock and Curly Dock (*Rumex* spp.)**, and Burdock** (*Arctium* spp.) The dock family is distributed all over the world and is a good green for salads and cooking. The leaves are best in spring or when the plants are young (they can appear all through the growing season). In Japan, burdock is known as *gobo*. It is a significant vegetable in many Asian countries including Korea and China. Burdock root is very nutritious and is a good source of potassium, calcium, and amino acids. In Chinese traditional medicine, burdock is used as a blood-purifying tonic and is also thought to promote healthy skin and hair.

Broadleaf dock (*Rumex obtusifolius*) leaves are elliptical when young and mature into a long arrow-shaped leaf. The mature leaves are very bitter. Broadleaf dock can be used interchangeably with curly dock (*Rumex crispus*), which is distinguished by the curly edge to the leaf. There is, however, a significant amount of variation in leaf size and shape between the two plants.

Dock leaves (particularly the tips) and seeds are edible. It is interesting to note that dock seeds are toxic to poultry in large doses. To prepare the leaves, strip the green from the stem (much like you would prepare kale), chop, and sauté or blanch. The flavour is fairly dominant, similar to Swiss chard, and is often used in a blend of milder, cooked wild greens.

Burdock (*Arctium lappa*) is a larger plant that shoots up stalks topped with burrs. The taproot is the prize; you must dig to remove the whole root. The deep root may go down into the soil for more than 24 inches (60 cm). Burdock is distinguished from common dock by the presence of fuzzy white hairs on the underside of the burdock leaf.

Chickweed (*Stellaria media*) Chickweed is a very common plant that has widespread distribution. The plant has oval to triangular leaves and pretty white flowers. The stem has a distinctive row of hairs on one side. When the conditions are right, the plant can form huge ground cover "carpets" that sprout in the early spring and may reseed and continue producing throughout the growing season. Chickweed has a mild flavour, is packed full of nutrition, and is an excellent source of vitamins and phytonutrients. Chickweed prefers acidic soils but can often be found growing wild in both gardens and in the cracks of sidewalks. There is a long list of ailments that the chickweed is prescribed for. It is a general body tonic with positive effects on your digestive and immune system.

For the best tasting chickweed, harvest only the top 2 inches (5 cm) of the plant. As the plant matures the lower stem becomes stringy and has a pronounced hay flavour. If you harvest a patch you can just trim off the edges with a pair of scissors. You may come back and repeatedly harvest the same patch.

Caution: Poisonous Look-Alike!

A plant called Scarlet pimpernel (*Anagallis arvensis*) appears similar to chickweed. Pimpernel has reddish flowers and smooth stems. Chickweed has white flowers and small hairs on the stems.

Common Cattail (*Typha latifolia*) This is a plant with many food uses, and there is evidence that early humans ate this plant as many as 30,000 years ago. It has edible parts that can be harvested throughout the year and consequently was an important plant for early foragers.

Traditionally, the roots were used by First Nations peoples and ground into nutrient-dense flour. The ripe cattail heads were ground and used as a thickening and binding flour. Today, the tender bases of the leaves continue to be eaten raw or cooked and are delicious. The green flower spikes can be boiled or baked and eaten. In the fall the roots become very starchy and can be pounded in water. The starch will drop to the bottom and can be drained and dried out to form a protein-rich powder.

Cattail is found in many locations where water is present, such as in lakes, swamps, ditches, etc. However, you must be careful to look for nearby external sources of pollution and contamination.

Dandelion (*Taraxacum officinale*) Dandelion is a very common inhabitant of both urban and rural areas. It was introduced as a pot-herb by immigrants and took off in a mad dash around the continent. Dandelion leaves are distinguished by the jagged downward-toothed edges (looking like lions' teeth). The young greens are very nutritious and tender in the spring. Dandelions will always have some component of bitterness and they become increasingly bitter as they mature. Exposure to sunlight is a key factor in developing these bitter compounds. Dandelions that grow in areas that are shaded have milder tasting leaves. In addition, greens that grow rapidly (for example, in the rich soil of a garden) also tend to be better choices for the table. The young leaves are eaten as salad greens or cooked greens. Harvest the young leaves at the core of the plant for best results.

Cooking tends to slightly lessen the bitterness of the leaves and allows you to add components to balance the flavour (for example, salt, garlic, lemon, etc). The plant is used medicinally to aid digestion and to treat certain skin conditions. It has laxative and diuretic effects.

The whole plant has been used in many forms for centuries. The unopened flower heads are particularly delicious. The flowers are made into wine and dried for tea. The root is roasted to make a beverage or infused to make salves and balms for skin ailments. The best part of the plant may be the crown of younger plants. This is the whitish centre of the plant from which the flower stock of the plant will shoot up. It is tender and aromatic and makes a nice addition to a stir-fry or an intriguing pickle.

Daylily (*Hemerocallis fulva* and other species) The most common variant is the Orange Daylily. It is a plant that originated in China and was introduced and spread around the planet. The plant is distinguished by the beautiful orange flowers and multiple slim flower buds. The leaves are used in Chinese cooking and medicine where they are known as "golden needles." There are many colour variations to the daylilies. The unopened flowers are referred to as buds and are excellent in stir-fries or eaten raw in salads.

There are other true lilies in the Pacific Northwest (*Lilium* spp.). These occur in forest and alpine areas. Many of these plants are sensitive to harvest and some are endangered. I do not recommend foraging for these lilies.

Field Mustard (*Brassica rapa*) Mustard is a very common plant of our fields and roadsides. Anywhere the soils are disturbed, wild mustard can take hold. There are several variants in the *Brassica* family that appear and most are interchangeable. You will probably first recognize the plant when in flower with bright yellow petals on a long, upright stalk. The leaves are lobed with a toothed edge, and there are often smaller lobes off-shooting from the base of bigger leaves. It is related to the radish and turnip families.

The leaves are tasty in the spring for salads or cooking, and the flower tops can be used as a vegetable. Once the plant flowers, edible seedpods develop. When the pods dry out and mature, they will contain reddish-brown mustard seeds.

Fireweed (*Chamerion angustifolium*) Fireweed is a tall and elegant plant that forms long clusters of flowers with four purple petals. The name *fireweed* comes from the plant's tendency to be the first to sprout up after an area has been burned. They also like damp areas and frequently line ditches and fields in the region. The tender shoots are edible and have a pleasant mild flavour. The plant flowers in late spring and early summer. The leaves are long and narrow. Beekeepers rely on the flowers to feed their forest edge beehives. Fireweed honey is one of the best in the Pacific Northwest.

Fireweed was an important spring food for First Nations. The young leaves were used as a salad or cooked with other greens. The inner parts of the stem are sweet and were often scraped off with the teeth. The young shoots were made into a tea and were believed to be a health tonic and blood purifier.

Fireweed is an excellent source of vitamins C and A. Ointment made from the plant is used as a balm to sooth irritated skin. Harvest the young leaves and sprouts in the spring. In the summer, you can eat the unopened flower buds as a vegetable.

Lamb's Quarters, or Wild Spinach (*Chenopodium album*) This plant is a common urban and countryside weed. It is recognized by its tall and majestic stature. When the plant flowers, it is distinguished by a silver to pink blush around the centre of the flower. Lamb's quarters is another powerhouse of nutrients and vitamins. The leaves are an excellent source of potassium, calcium, and manganese with very high levels of vitamins (K, A, and C). It is renowned as a general body tonic and helps boost the immune system and metabolism.

When mature, the leaves contain higher levels of sodium and oxalic acid (linked to kidney stones). You should be cautious with this plant if you have a history of issues with kidney stones. The young leaves should be eaten (in moderation) in the spring, as the plant also becomes bitter as it ages. The seeds are highly nutritious (related to quinoa), and both the leaves and seeds are used extensively in Indian cuisine (where it is called *bathua*).

The whole plant can be eaten during most of its growing life. The young leaves are fresh and green tasting in a salad, and the larger leaves can be cooked like spinach. The flower tops can be cooked and eaten as a vegetable. And the seeds can be used much like quinoa. Soak the seeds before cooking to remove a little of the bitterness.

Caution: Poisonous Look-Alike!

Hairy nightshade (*Solanum sarrachoides*) can look very similar to lamb's quarters. The difference is nightshade has small hairs on the stem and leaves and has a large white flower whereas lamb's quarters has a powdery (actually waxy) dusting on the centre of the growing tips and is hairless. When lamb's quarters is mature, it produces green flower buds that contain reddish-brown seeds.

Mallow (*Malva neglecta*) A common and widely distributed plant, mallow is similar in shape to the common geranium and sports beautiful white-and-pink flowers. Its cousin marsh mallow (*Althaea officinalis*) is often grown as a garden plant and has frequently escaped and populated the wild. Both plants contain a gelling agent that thickens foods into stable foam. They were initially used to make the famous namesake marshmallow (which is today made primarily with gelatin).

Mallow grows in rich, compact soil and is common on the fringes of civilization. The leaves are edible and are usually cooked to make the texture a little more palatable. They have a beautiful, geometric shape with folds extending out from the centre of the leaf to create a ruffled edge. If using the leaves raw, soak in water to rehydrate. They will quickly wilt if left out to dry. The leaves make great tempura. The flowers are white with pink blushes or lines. Once the plant flowers, there are small fruits or peas that form. The peas are edible and are a rich source of the thickening (mucilaginous) qualities as the leaves and stems. The peas can be added to soups and stew for a similar effect to okra.

WILD MINT

Miner's Lettuce (*Claytonia perfoliata*) This might be one of my favourite springtime greens. It is an introduced plant that has widespread range in our region. It grows under mature trees and lines ditches and wet areas. The leaves are triangular to start and round as they mature. The plant flowers from the centre of the leaf, producing a short stem and a delicate white flower. The flavour is mild, spinach-like with a slightly citrus flavour. The greens are a wonderful addition to a salad bowl. The plant is a good source of vitamin C and an excellent source of plant protein and fibre.

The plant is one of the first to sprout in the spring and creates large and spectacular masses of greenery. Once temperatures rise and the rainfalls diminish, the plant withers and dies, eventually disappearing to then be replaced by other wild plants. The stem is tender and the plant is easily harvested by pinching off the flower at the stem. The leaves are not bitter and are excellent even after the plant has flowered. Miner's lettuce is best eaten raw and can form the mild base of a delicious wild foods salad. It is also a great green to purée into smoothies. When the plants are mature with long stems, I like to chop the stems and leaves and quickly sauté with garlic for a tasty vegetable.

Mint (*Mentha arvensis*) Wild mint is common in the wet areas and fields of the region. You might notice it when the plant flowers in the summer. The purple-blue flowers are very pretty and tend to produce short spikes of colour often in a sea of green. The plant is most tender in the early summer and becomes more intensely minty as the summer progresses. Wild mint is strongly flavoured and has a slight bitter edge. It makes an excellent tea and is a nice addition to salads.

Oxeye Daisy (*Leucanthemum vulgare*) This daisy is a common wildflower that is abundant in fields and along roadsides in the region. The white petals and yellow centre are very visible in the summer when the plant flowers by the thousands. The leaves in the spring are one of the best edibles available, growing as a rosette of green, beautifully cut leaves. The flavour is reminiscent of green apples and sage with a sweet aftertaste. Add young leaves to salad mixes or mix into dressing and sauces. A tea from the leaves can be used as a mild, relaxing tonic.

As the plant matures, a green flower stem shoots up with a tightly closed emerging flower head. The whole shoot is edible and tasty as a vegetable or soup herb. The flower buds resemble caper berries and can be pickled. Once the flower opens up, the petals can be used in salads and dried for tea. The greens become bitter once the plant flowers and have a very pungent and somewhat overpowering aroma. The mature leaves were traditionally used as an insect repellant.

Pineapple Weed (*Matricaria discoidea*) The aromatic flower is cone shaped and lacks any petals. The flowers are used to make a soothing tea and can be used to flavour a wide range of dressings and even baked goods. The tea is reputed to be soothing for a cold and helps aid digestion and calm an upset stomach. It also has strong anti-bacterial properties and is reputed to have anti-inflammatory effects.

The plant favours the edges of inhabited areas and likes to pop up in compacted soil. The plant first flowers in hot weather and will keep growing throughout the warm months. Harvest the plant by removing the tips of the cone-shaped flowers and leaves. The flowers are great in salads and can also be pickled or preserved in syrup. The flowers are excellent dried and will make a wonderful tea—one of the best in fact.

Purslane (*Portulaca oleracea*) Purslane is a succulent plant that loves the hot weather. It occurs in summer and is rich in flavour. The leaves are tender and exceptionally high in minerals and omega-3 fatty acids. Purslane is an excellent source of antioxidants and deserves to be more widely known. It is used in traditional Chinese medicine to combat infections and can be applied to insect bites to stop the itching.

The young leaves have a reddish tinge and are very plump. The plant has a branching structure that tends to spread quickly over the ground. The plant produces a small yellow flower that will produce a tiny, cup-like structure filled with seeds. The tender stems and leaves are edible. The tips and leaves are great in a salad; the whole plant is great as a cooked vegetable and has a pleasant, sour flavour and soft, gelatinous texture. Blanch the leaves in boiling salted water for 2 to 3 minutes, then refresh in cold water. The blanched leaves can also be puréed into sauces and soups.

Sheep Sorrel (*Rumex acetosella*) Sorrel has a pleasant sour taste that is used to provide tartness to dishes and is used as a curdling agent when making some types of cheese. Medicinally, the plant was an important First Nations herb used for treating

A.

B.

C.

inflammation, fevers, and digestive issues. It is considered to be a whole body tonic and useful for detoxification and cell regeneration.

It is a cousin of the dock family of greens and both are related to wild buckwheat. The plant flowers with tall, reddish spikes that are very common in fields and at the edges of forests. The leaves are lance shaped with small spikes at the base of the leaf (making it look like a little rocket). It reproduces by seed and by sending out rhizomes. This makes the plant difficult to remove from gardens and has ensured the plant is widely available throughout the growing season.

When harvesting sorrel, look for large, healthy clumps and cut with a pair of scissors. Back in the kitchen, soak in water and spin dry. Remove the tough stems and use leaves in salads or as an herb for seasoning.

Stinging Nettle (*Urtica dioica*) A common plant in this region, nettle is identified by its sharply serrated edges. The leaves grow in opposite pairs on either side of the hairy stem of the plant. It favours moist areas at the edges of roads and trails and is often seen in the rich soils near barnyards. Nettle often forms in large banks of leaves. To protect yourself when picking nettles, wear garden gloves and use a pair of scissors. Pick just the top tips of the plant and the first pair of good leaves on the stalk, before the plant has a chance to flower. When the plant is mature, it grows tiny crystals that are irritating to the digestive system. When you get home, wash the nettles in cold water and drain before using them in cooking.

Stinging nettles contain histamines. They have many therapeutic properties and are taken to treat allergies. They are also a popular folk remedy for arthritis. The leaves are rich in vitamin C and A and are good sources of iron, potassium, manganese, and calcium. The leaves are a very good source of protein. The young leaf tops dry well and are often used to make a therapeutic tea. Blanch nettles in boiling water to remove the stinging qualities. They can then be frozen for storage for several months.

Sweet Cicely (*Osmorhiza longistylis*) The plant displays beautiful, fern-like leaves with the faint scent of anise. This is another introduced plant that has found a home in the Pacific Northwest. Look for sweet cicely in moist, wooded areas. The plant flowers with large, multi-flowered white blossoms that turn into long elliptical seeds. The seedpods

A. PINEAPPLE WEED B. DAYLILY C. MALLOW LEAF

have a strong anise flavour when fresh. They dry out quickly and the flavour diminishes. The roots have the same strong, licorice flavour and can be used in savoury and sweet dishes. Leaves, seeds, and roots can be dried to make a fine addition to tea mixes.

Wild Onion, especially the Nodding Onion (*Allium cernuum*) Wild onions are found in coastal valleys and open forest meadows. I look for moist areas that get access to sunshine. There is a characteristic onion odour that often is apparent before you see the plant. The nodding onion is named for its habit of drooping (or nodding) toward the ground. The flowers are white or pink and form seed heads.

The onion bulb and leaves are sweetest in spring, becoming quite strong flavoured as the season progresses. First Nations loved to roast the bulbs in fire pits; the roasted bulbs were served to important visitors.

Wild Roses (*Rosa* spp.) The flowers, leaves (when young), and hips are all edible. The leaves and hips are rich in vitamins C, A, and E. The plant is easily recognizable and is considered a prime food for survival situations. There has been much recent research into the promising anti-cancer properties of the rose and the plant is often used as part of a detoxifying program.

The flowers bloom in late May and soon drop their petals to reveal green seedpods called hips. Over the following months the hips ripen and turn reddish orange. Harvest after the first frost for the sweetest rosehip flesh. The interior contains tiny hairs that must be strained out of any product made for consumption. The hairs are very irritating to the digestive system.

3) Deciduous Trees

Leaf-bearing trees bring us many wonderful foods—apples, pears, stone fruits, and plums are the most common. They have also escaped captivity and many wild versions exist in our region and throughout the world. I could fill a boot just on the product of trees but instead offer a few of my favourite local wild products.

Bigleaf Maple (*Acer macrophyllum*) Western maples are majestic trees that can grow to 65 feet (20 m) tall. They are also home to lush carpets of moss that often line the trunks.

WILD ONION

A.

B.

C.

The licorice fern (a fern with an edible root) likes to grow out of these moss patches.

In December through February, the trees are tapped for a distinctive syrup. It takes 60 to 70 quarts (60–70 L) of sap to make 1 quart (1 L) of syrup. The syrup is delicious with a slight mineral and acidic edge that makes it stand out from traditional maple syrup. In the spring, the tree flowers and the flowers can be eaten or used to infuse syrups. I have also cooked the blossoms into fritters or tempura. In the fall, the maples form keys (seeds) that can be boiled and eaten as a snack.

Crabapple (*Malus* spp.) Tucked into gardens and forest edges, the crabapple is a common wild plant and ornamental in many old farmyards and gardens. The fruit is small and often sour or bitter. Cooking transforms it into something special and the crabapple has a significant quantity of pectin, making it a good fruit to mix with wild berries to create beautiful jellies.

Use the crabapple in baking as you would a regular apple; they just need a little extra sweetening to compensate for the bitter and tannic edge. They are excellent pickled with spices and a stick or two of cinnamon.

Hazelnut (*Corylus cornuta*) The hazelnut is a common native tree in the region and (some, like my dog Oliver, say unfortunately) a favourite food of squirrels. The tree forms bushes and trees up to 18 feet (6 m) in height. The nuts are fully formed by August and can be eaten raw or allowed to dry in the shell before shucking. Roasting the nuts brings out deep, rich flavours. The tree bark has been traditionally used as a soothing tonic for sore throats and upset stomachs. Local First Nations picked the nuts and dried them out for winter use. They were most often eaten raw.

Plum (*Prunus* spp.) There are lots of wild plum trees dotting the landscape. Most are introduced species from Europe and Asia. You often don't see the tree until it blooms with a profusion of white or pink blossoms in the spring. A common variety is the Japanese plum (*Prunus salicina*), which is found along pathways and streams in our region. The wild plums are small and tart with a sweet finish when ripe. The fruit may be yellow or reddish and may darken to deep purple when ripe. The fruit can be processed into preserves or jelly, or used to infuse alcohol with a fine plum flavour.

A. LICORICE FERN LEAVES B. MOSS ON BIGLEAF MAPLE C. HAZELNUTS

Sumac (*Rhus typhina* or *R. glabra*) The sumac plant is most noticeable in summer when it flowers in a deep red cone. The staghorn sumac (*R. typhina*) is grown as an ornamental all over the world and has escaped into the countryside. Sumac flowers are harvested in late summer and early fall when they have a fine lemony acidity. The dried flowers are used to make a kind of lemonade-like drink. In the Middle East, sumac is used as a seasoning, most famously as the tart component of the spice mix called za'atar.

Caution: Poisonous Look-Alike!

There is a bad cousin of the edible sumac, commonly called poison sumac (*Toxicodendron vernix*). It displays white berries and should be easy to distinguish and avoid.

4) Coniferous Trees

Most of the region's fir, spruce, and pine trees are edible. The needles make an acceptable tea and have been used as medicinal ingredients for centuries. The raw needles contain significant levels of vitamin C and a tea made from the needles is soothing to sore throats and helps open up the airways if you are suffering from congestion. My personal favourite is the grand fir, followed closely by Douglas fir.

Douglas Fir (*Pseudotsuga menziesii*) The Douglas fir is a magnificent tree any way you look at it. It is often the tree making up the giant, old-growth forests of the northern coast. The biggest tree recorded is over 350 feet (over 105 m). Douglas firs can obtain diameters approaching 16 feet (about 4.9 m). They are important trees for mushroom foraging, hosting a variety of edible fungi in their root systems. The leaves are also highly aromatic and can be used in teas, infusions, and broths.

Grand Fir (*Abies grandis*) This tree reminds me of the Christmases of my youth. Later, I discovered it was a wonderful aromatic and a fine addition to food and drinks. I often serve grand fir tea to guests, surprising them with the fine and delicate flavour.

The tree is a tall, majestic specimen that can reach heights topping 200 feet (60 m). The needles are distinctive in that they branch out flatly from the branch. Each tip is slightly notched and the backside of the needle has a green strip bound by white strips above and below.

In the spring, the new tips are soft and highly aromatic. They are used to infuse honey, syrup, vinegar, and oil. I also process the new tips with sea salt to preserve the essential oils and make a lovely green salt for curing and seasoning food. The needles are edible year-round and make an acceptable tea year-round.

Sitka Spruce (*Picea sitchensis*) The Sitka is another magnificent tree of the coast. It rivals the Douglas fir in size and specimens have reached over 300 feet (over 90 m) in height. The needles are like a typical spruce and very stiff. The needles will hurt if tapped into your skin. In the spring, the new shoots are soft and can be used to infuse syrups and prepare essential oils.

5) Mushrooms

We live in a magical place for mushrooms. The Pacific Northwest is washed with warm rains from the Pacific and our temperate climate is perfect for the production of mushrooms. Our mushrooms are often known for the gigantic size they can reach, with many of the largest specimens on the planet recorded in our forests and fields. The chanterelle is the most abundant of the species and the prime mushroom for beginners to seek out.

Mushrooms have complex relationships with trees and the environment. They are critical to the health of our planet and play an important role in keeping the world growing and composting the remains when the growth finally ends. The science of fungi is continually evolving. Techniques like DNA analysis have been used to help identify and classify mushrooms. Many new species have been added or names changed in recent times. This means that many old field books may not have current information on the mushroom and in some cases the edibility of some mushrooms has been brought into question. One example is the honey mushroom (*Armillaria mellea*). A mushroom that was frequently eaten and listed as edible, it is now thought to cause kidney damage if eaten in large quantities over a number of years. A little will probably not hurt you, but a steady diet of honey mushrooms is probably not wise.

There are many mushroom species out there. Some estimates are in the range of 10,000 species for the Pacific Northwest. Only a select few are edible (maybe 50 species). This leaves a lot of mushrooms that you should avoid. The best advice is keep to a small group of fungi that you can confidently identify and leave the rest in the forests and fields. Chanterelles and morels are relatively easy to identify and occur in some abundance. That's a good place to start your mushroom-foraging journey.

Chanterelles The chanterelle family includes many strange and wonderfully coloured fungi, from pale, creamy white to psychedelic shades of electric blue. Yellow chanterelles are abundant in the Pacific Northwest, where the forests often provide bumper crops. On many occasions, I have encountered several hundred chanterelles over the course of a short hike. This abundance has led to increased availability in public markets and specialty stores; chanterelles are continually gaining wider exposure. Dry chanterelles are a step down in quality from fresh as the drying process renders the mushroom very tough, with a slightly bitter and peppery taste. Frozen chanterelles are a good addition to soups and stews.

The yellow chanterelle is probably the best mushroom with which to start your foraging career. It is fairly easy to identify, abundant, and the mushrooms that look like it won't kill you (always a bonus). The chanterelle exists over most of the temperate zones of the planet. It is beloved in Europe, Asia, North America, South America, and South Africa. The chanterelle also happens to taste great, making it a good mushroom to get to know.

Yellow Chanterelle, or Pacific Golden Chanterelle (*Cantharellus formosus* and other species) Chanterelles are many people's favourite wild mushroom. They have a beautiful elegant form, are plentiful, and are unique in several characteristics. The bright yellow-orange colour also allows them to stick out from the forest floor.

The chanterelle really likes locations with a deep, lush carpet of moss along with a fairly mature canopy of trees. I've had great success in older, second-growth forests and mature (15–20 year), third-growth forests. Find one chanterelle and a careful search will usually turn up more hiding under the surrounding trees. In France, a smaller variety of chanterelle is known as the girolle (*Cantharellus cibarius*). These may also occur in eastern North America. Our Pacific variety is known for its huge size and paler underside. There is a second, large Pacific Northwest variety called *Cantharellus cascadensis*. It is very similar to the *C. formosus*, with a slightly brighter yellow cap and a thin, wavy edge. A third local variant is the *C. cibarius* var. *roseocanus*. It is the smallest, but most fragrant,

A. WHITE CHANTERELLES B. PORCINI C. LOBSTER MUSHROOMS

A.

B.

of the yellow chanterelles found in the Pacific Northwest. Look for chanterelles in flat, forested areas at the base of hills and along the slopes. The chanterelle tends to fruit under Douglas fir trees in the Pacific Northwest.

White Chanterelle (*Cantharellus subalbidus*) This delicious chanterelle is a cousin of the yellow chanterelle. The colour is pale white to cream when fresh. After picking, the mushrooms often discolour around the edges and the flesh appears to be slightly bruised in darker shades of orange. The stem of the white chanterelle is often much thicker than the common yellow varieties. The flesh is tender and mild and it is one of my favourite mushrooms for chowders and soups. The white chanterelle is often found in great numbers. The flesh can become saturated if there is too much moisture and they are sometimes attacked by fungus gnats and moulds near the end of the season. The white chanterelle does not like cold temperatures and will quickly rot if frozen. Look for white chanterelles at the edges of forests and in stands of salal and ferns.

Winter Chanterelle, Yellow Foot Chanterelle, or Funnel Chanterelle (*Craterellus tubae-formis*) The funnel chanterelle is a common late-season mushroom, particularly after heavy rains. It was formerly called the *Cantharellus tubaeformis*. The mushroom has a delicate, funnel-shaped cap that is hollow in the middle. The stem of the mushroom is yellow and hollow. Look for this mushroom growing near or on rotting wood.

They are tasty sautéed and are often found in dried mushroom mixtures (particularly from France). This delicate mushroom quickly loses its shape after picking and can degenerate into a soggy, larva-infected mass if not stored properly. Wrap the mushrooms in plenty of paper towels, and refrigerate in a container that provides lots of side ventilation. Drying the mushroom actually helps to concentrate the flavour and results in a pleasing, firm texture. Locally, we find the winter chanterelle among the Douglas fir and hemlock trees.

Morels Morels are delicious fresh or dried, and are considered one of the top culinary mushrooms. They should always be eaten cooked, as the raw mushrooms can cause allergic reactions in many people.

A. BLACK MORELS B. HEDGEHOG MUSHROOMS

Morels are sometimes difficult to forage because they tend to blend in with the surrounding landscape. The morel has a distinctive cone shape that is often pointed. The surface resembles a sponge with lots of ridges and wrinkles. In an average spring, morels will appear soon after the crocus flowers bloom. Thousands of morels often sprout the year following a forest fire. Morels seem to like disturbances and often sprout from road cuts, excavations, and fallen trees.

The classification of morels is very complex and has undergone much revision in the last few years. The following are the region's most common species.

Black Morel (*Morchella elata* and other species) The black morel is one of the first morels to appear in the spring. The black varieties are particularly difficult to see in the forest. The head looks almost identical to a fallen pinecone. To successfully forage for the black morel, you often have to key on sighting the white stem and then focus in on the black cap of the mushroom. The morel occurs early in the spring and may be present well into summer. The black morel can also occur in high alpine meadows, fruiting much later than morels at a lower altitude. Look for the black morel under conifers, poplars, and shrub undergrowth. Morels seem to particularly like to fruit under aspen and pine trees but are found in a wide range of habitat.

Common Morel (*Morchella esculenta* and other species) Common morels fruit after the black morel and can fruit in huge numbers if the conditions are right. They are often found at lower elevations than other morels. They are similar in structure to the black morel, but with the surface looking grey to dull yellow, as opposed to black. The common morel prefers the late spring and needs a long warm spell of weather after a particularly cold winter. It seems to be partial to apple and cherry orchards, as well as aspen forests, but they also appear in a wide variety of habitats.

Burnsite Morel (*Morchella tomentosa* and other species) A West Coast variation of the black morel, the burnsite morel occurs up to two years after a forest fire, usually reproducing in prolific amounts. These morels appear similar to the black and common varieties and are basically distinguished by the habitat in which they are found. New DNA evidence

A. MIXED HARVEST OF WILD MUSHROOMS B. PINE MUSHROOM CLOSEUP C. CAULIFLOWER FUNGUS

A.

B.

C.

has greatly reorganized the entire category of morels. It is thought these morels are the first to return after a fire to take advantage of the lack of competition from other mushrooms. The morels also feed on the burnt plant materials of the forest floor and help recycle the nutrients. These morels will have a distinct smoky flavour, particularly when dried.

Western Blond Morel (*Morchella frustrata*) This morel is a recent addition to the scientific catalogue. It is related to the common morel but differs in subtle anatomical details. The western blond morel is one of the tastiest members of the morel family. It is distinguished by the pale white-yellow surface of the mushroom. It is often significantly more rounded than the pointed black and common morels. Locally, it can grow to gigantic proportions, making one mushroom a good part of meal. I have foraged several specimens that weighed over 1 pound (454 g) each. The western blond morel seems to like steep slopes and plateaus. It also likes older growth forests of conifer trees and patches of disturbed soil.

Other Species Recommended for Mushroom Foraging There are thought to be about 10,000 species of mushrooms in the Pacific Northwest. A few are poisonous and most are of no value for collecting for the tables. Outside of chanterelles and morels, the risk of misidentification increases. However, there are a few species that are particularly tasty and worth getting to know.

Cauliflower Fungus (*Sparassis crispa*) This is a unique, large fungus that looks like a compact bunch of ribbons. It's common name, cauliflower mushroom, comes from its passing resemblance to this great garden vegetable. This mushroom, however, will be found growing on a dead tree and not in your garden. Though not common, this is an excellent find particularly since one mushroom may weigh several pounds. Soak the whole mushroom in a solution of cold water and salt to rid it of any insect visitors. The aroma is very appealing and the crisp texture makes it one of the best edible mushrooms. Look for the fungus growing at the base of rotting Douglas fir stumps.

Field Mushrooms (various *Agaricus* species) Similar to the store-bought common white button mushroom, wild field mushrooms are common and an excellent find.

Be very careful to distinguish the mushroom from the entire *Amanita* family. If there is any doubt, do not consume the mushrooms. Many poisonings are due to confusion over these two mushroom families. The undercap of the field mushroom should be pink when young, changing to chocolate brown as the mushroom matures. Do not pick button mushrooms with white or yellow gills. Look for field mushrooms in grassy meadows, particularly where animals are grazing. Be particularly careful when identifying *Agaricus* mushrooms in the forest or at the edge of fields.

Caution: Poisonous Look-Alike!

Destroying Angel (*Amanita ocreata*) and Death Cap (*Amanita phalloides*): Young *Amanita* buttons look similar to young *Agaricus* mushrooms. *A. ocreata* is native to the Pacific Northwest but rare in British Columbia. It contains deadly amatoxins. Poisoning symptoms include vomiting and intestinal issues that begin 2 to 3 days after consumption. Unfortunately internal damage continues and compromises the function of the kidney and liver for the next 5 to 6 days. *A. phalloides* is a European species that has been introduced into North America. It is out there and does poison people. It will have an olive green hue to the cap. When young, the amanitas appear egg shaped and are covered by a thin veil of tissue. There are other lots of other amanitas to be careful about.

Hedgehog Mushroom (*Hydnum repandum*) At first glance, this mushroom looks like a large chanterelle. The underside of the cap has a shredded appearance that resembles a tiny shag carpet. The flesh is firm and dense and is quite delicious in soups or stews. It makes a good dried mushroom. Look for hedgehog mushrooms in the same terrain as chanterelles. They do tend to like the bottom of valleys and vales, particularly if there is water nearby.

Lobster Mushroom (*Hypomyces lactifluorum*) A vivid red-orange mushroom, this fungus is a joint effort between a host mushroom (usually a *Russula brevipes* or *R. cascadensis* in our area) and a parasite that attacks and transforms the host into an excellent edible mushroom. Guidebooks warn that sometimes the host mushroom can be poisonous. Pickers should identify the mushrooms surrounding the lobster

A.

B.

C.

mushroom to identify the host. The lobster mushroom has a crusty, florescent orange exterior, firm flesh, and a sweet flavour. The host mushroom is usually a large white, gilled mushroom before its transformation.

> **Caution: Identify the host mushrooms surrounding the lobster mushrooms.** Only pick the lobster mushroom if you can confidently identify the host mushroom as non-poisonous.

Oyster Mushroom (*Pleurotus* spp.) The oyster mushroom is typically a white to light grey, fan-shaped mushroom. It grows on dead deciduous trees (usually alder locally). The mushroom grows in clumps on broken trees and on deadfall near the banks of streams and rivers. The oyster mushroom is a good mushroom for the beginning forager because it is abundant and relatively safe to collect.

Pine Mushroom, or Matsutake (*Tricholoma magnivelare*) The mushroom has a firm, dense flesh and a spicy aroma that is reminiscent of cinnamon. The scent is a key factor in determining the identity of the pine mushroom. Look for the pine mushroom in higher altitudes in stands of mature Douglas fir and hemlock. At lower elevations, they occur in stands of pine and huckleberry. In the Pacific Northwest, the mushroom starts fruiting in late September and continues on until the first hard frosts (usually about mid-November). Once you have smelled a fresh pine mushroom, you may find the scent intoxicating. Unfortunately, this volatile aroma is largely lost when the mushroom is dried or frozen. Pine mushrooms can be used like truffles to infuse flavour into a wide variety of dishes.

> **Caution: Poisonous Look-Alike!**
> Smith's amanita (*Amanita smithiana*) is very similar in appearance (as a small button), but the odour is not spicy. The mushroom can be pure white or with powdery scales on top. There is a shaggy fringe on the edge of the cap, extending to veil under the cap. It is also an imposing mushroom; it can be up to 8 inches (20 cm) tall. The spores and spore print will be white.

Porcini, or Cep (*Boletus edulis*) The porcini is characterized by a fat, light-brown top and a distinctive swollen base. There is some debate over the species name of our

A. MUSHROOM HARVEST B. WILD OYSTER MUSHROOMS C. CLEANED PINE MUSHROOM BUTTONS

Pacific Northwest porcini. There may in fact be a different species that is yet to be determined. When the mushroom is young, the undercap will be whitish and firm. As it ages, it becomes yellow, darkening to green, and finally brown when it begins to break down. Also look for small pinholes in the sponge, signs that worms have penetrated the flesh.

Soft-fleshed porcini are often bitter and have a slimy texture. Firm small porcini (buttons) freeze well. Cook them partially frozen for the best results. Look for the porcini in two habitats: near the ocean at the top of beaches in the undergrowth and on the slopes and high alpine areas, particularly near lakes and streams.

THE SEASHORE

6) Sea Vegetables

Foraging on the seashore has been an important tool for humanity since the dawn of civilization. Seaweeds in particular are incredibly nutritious, abundant, and relatively easy to forage. The spring is best for many types of seaweed, but many are available year-round on our coast. Picking seaweed dislodged by tides and waves is the most sustainable way to harvest sea vegetables. Many are available in the intertidal zone that is exposed with the tides. Offshore kelp forests are important sanctuaries for fish and animals and therefore should be only selectively harvested, if at all. Most varieties of seaweed are also commercially available in stores as dried (and occasionally fresh) products. These products are often farmed and produced using sustainable processes.

Seaweed can begin to rot once it is removed from the ocean and allowed to warm up. Seaweed collected from dry beaches usually has a little stability. Seaweed harvested in ocean water should be kept moist until you can deal with it at home. I usually harvest small amounts moistened with seawater and transport them home in buckets to be processed in batches. Rinse kelp and *Alaria* (brown algae) in fresh water before drying. Laver and sea lettuce can be rinsed with salt water during harvesting.

Sea vegetables pack a lot into their small package—proteins, vitamins, and calcium are abundant. Seaweed is also reputed to help the body rid itself of toxins. Sodium alginate bonds with toxins and heavy metals and helps the body flush them from the system. Many seaweeds are edible raw and all make great dried product, reconstituting quickly to closely resemble the fresh product.

One brown seaweed, Flattened Acid Kelp (*Desmarestia ligulata*), releases sulfuric acid when removed from the ocean. It exists primarily in the lower tidal areas. This is one seaweed that obviously must not be collected.

Sea beans technically are land-based plants existing at the top of the intertidal zone. They are included in the sea vegetable category due to their ocean flavouring and high salt content.

***Alaria* Species, commonly California Wakame** (*Alaria marginata*) *Alaria* is the genus name for a number of brown algae. It is best harvested in the spring and fall. It is common on rocky shorelines and attaches to boulders and ledges. The seaweed has a distinctive brown, ruffled blade with a lighter brown stem running down the leaf. The leaf is broad and shaped like a fern or feather. Most blades are less than 3 feet (1 m) in length. In the water, the buoyant central shaft floats the alaria like a raft.

Alaria is tasty raw or lightly dressed with a vinaigrette. It is a great seaweed for cooking into sauces and soups.

Bull Kelp (*Nereocystis luetkeana* and many other species) Common seaweed, known as kelp, is often seen washed up on beaches after storms. The plant is fast growing and anchors itself to the bottom of the seabed, with long, smooth blades growing from a central float. The plant can be used in many forms. The long whips can be pickled. The leaves can be used to wrap fish and vegetables for roasting. The entire plant can be dried and ground into powder.

Several varieties of kelp form vast kelp forests found along the coast. These are important breeding grounds for fish as well as habitat and protection for many species of ocean life.

Purple Laver, or Nori (*Porphyra* spp.) Look for laver on the beach from the high tide mark down to the waterline. It is sometimes tangled in with bull kelp or stranded on intertidal ledges. Nori has a very fine texture and the surface feels slippery. The leaves appear shiny and are almost transparent if held up to the light. There are several varieties and structures present on our shores. It may appear reddish brown when wet and dries to a dark purple sheen.

The seaweed is excellent fresh in the spring and makes a wonderful dried seaweed cake. Local First Nations dried the seaweed in spring when it is at its prime. The seaweed was dried in cakes on racks over fires or woodstoves, imparting a subtle, smoked flavour to the seaweed. In Japan, fresh seaweed is dried in thin sheets, used often for sushi or garnishing many dishes. I like to dry the nori in thin sheets using a food dehydrator.

Sea Bean (*Salicornia* spp.) This plant is found at the top of beaches in the zone where the highest tides reach. Sea beans are best in the summer months when the stems are plump and tender, before the plant flowers. They tend to grow in large and vigorous patches through the warm months and die back in the winter. It is best to soak the sea beans in cold water to refresh and remove a little of the salt before processing. *Salicornia* makes a great vegetable or pickle. Sea beans will keep well for a week to 10 days in the refrigerator. You can also quickly blanch them in boiling water, chill, bag, and freeze for several months.

Sea Lettuce (*Ulva lactuca* and other species) Look for sea lettuce floating on still pools of seawater or clinging to rocks or other seaweed. The leaves are bright green and have a thin and translucent appearance. Sometimes there is a whitish margin to the leaves. Sea lettuce thrives in areas with high nutrient levels. The mature leaves will grow up to 3 feet (1 m) in length. It is best harvested in the spring. In the summer, sea lettuce often dies off and begins to rot.

7) Shellfish

Modern shellfish foraging is hampered by the fact that shellfish are very sensitive to pollution and contamination. Shellfish are filter feeders that tend to concentrate toxins and pollutants. They are also prone to contamination from natural phenomena like toxic algae blooms (see PSP, p. 11). These dangers lurk in shellfish that otherwise look healthy and taste fine. For these reasons, shellfish foraging is a relatively dangerous pastime that should only be undertaken in pristine areas, far from the influence of civilization and in areas that are not affected by shellfish bans.

Like many other wild foods, the most abundant products are those that are introduced species. The introduced species often flourish due to a lack of predators and a hardy constitution (needed to flourish in diverse environments). Many of the region's beaches are dominated by the clams (Manila) and mussels that were introduced to the West Coast by oyster growers attempting to grow Japanese oysters in our waters. The native shellfish sometimes struggle to compete and are found in very limited areas. Local shellfish have a checkered history in resource management. Delicacies like abalone were overfished to the extent the fishery collapsed and it has yet to be re-established.

For these and many other reasons, you might be wise to avoid the wild harvest of these products and enjoy the efforts of professional harvesters and shellfish aquaculture farms. Even so, it is highly educational to find and observe these products in the wild.

We are spoiled here on the West Coast in our bounty of amazing shellfish. The ocean waters flowing down the coast from northern climates are rich with nutrients and very cold. This creates prime areas for shellfish production around the mid-zone of Vancouver Island. Cold waters are necessary for fine flavours, and nutrients are necessary for rapid growth and healthy shellfish.

Shellfish aquaculture (unlike salmon farming) is an industry that has largely been deemed sustainable and causes little harmful impact to the local environment. Shellfish need clean, nutrient-filled water and not much else. They are, however, subject to the effects of dangers like pollution and red tide. Red tide is an interesting phenomenon. Also called Paralytic Shellfish Poisoning (or PSP, see p. 11), it is caused by a population explosion of tiny toxic plankton. Shellfish feed on these organisms and pass the effects on to the eater. When a Red Tide warning is posted, the harvest of shellfish is banned until the toxin levels are reduced to a safe level. All commercial shellfish in BC is tested to determine the safety of our products.

Shellfish were an important part of the local coastal First Nations diet. Recently, archaeologists discovered man-made terracing in clam-rich areas that have been termed "clam gardens." These were areas that captured fine sands and made a great habitat for several types of clams.

Clam (*Protothaca staminea* and many other species) Local clams were a special food source for the local First Nations peoples. They harvested many varieties of clams and cockles. Some were wind dried and kept for use in the winter, some were baked in fire pits covered with seaweed for use in celebrations and potlatch ceremonies.

Whole Geoduck Preparation

The geoduck clam may look like an imposing creature, but it is relatively straightforward to cook with.

Place the geoduck on a cutting board and run a knife between the shell and the body of the clam (this might release some moisture so have a towel nearby). Repeat with the second side of the shell. Run your knife along the shell to free the meat. You will see a large ball (stomach at the base of the clam neck). Cut off this piece and discard.

Bring a large stockpot filled with water to a boil. Add the geoduck clam and cook for 1 to 2 minutes. You will see the skin of the clam wrinkle and bubble. Remove the clam and place in a bowl with ice-cold water. When cool enough to handle, pick up the clam and peel off the outer skin (this should peel back easily).

Make an incision down the length of the clam neck and flatten into one piece. Using a sharp knife, cut thin slices off the clam (go on a slight diagonal to make thin, wide slices).

Most of the clams we see on the beaches today are Manila clams (*Venerupis philippinarum*), an introduced species that is known for its tender meat and small size. These clams are now found wild all over the coast and appear to have adapted well to our climate. The other common clams include butter clams (*Saxidomus gigantea*), cockles (*Clinocardium* spp.), and razor clams (*Siliqua patula*).

The Manila and littleneck (*Protothaca staminea*) clams appear high up on the beaches (the top third during low tide). If you are lucky enough to find a mud and gravel beach, the clams may be lurking only inches below the surface. Butter clams are a little farther down the tide line and can be buried up to 12 inches (30 cm) below the surface.

Of special interest is the geoduck clam (*Panopea generosa*). The common name comes from the First Nations phrase for "dig deep" and this massive clam is the king of the intertidal zone. Most modern harvesting is done by divers with hoses blowing seawater into the soft sediments to dislodge the clam. Geoducks are farmed by seeding the clams into appropriate foreshore. It does take up to 12 years to mature the clam to market sizes. Some geoducks are incredibly long lived, with some specimens living for over 100 years. The geoduck clam is highly valued in Asian cultures and is truly an impressive specimen.

A. SEAWEED B. JAPANESE OYSTER C. MUSSELS AND BARNACLES

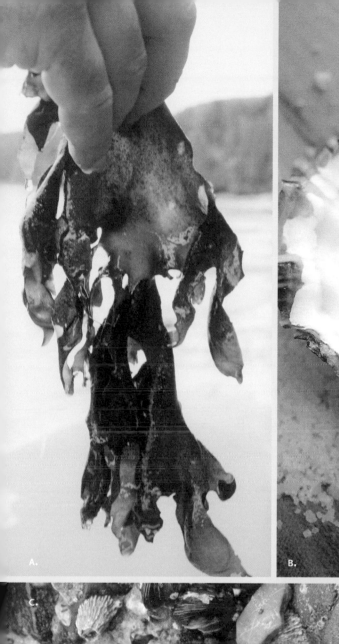

A.

B.

C.

Gooseneck Barnacle (*Pollicipes polymerus*) Let's face it, these are bizarre-looking creatures. When I first encountered them in Spain, I thought I was looking at some alien creature. One bite and I was convinced, converted to a barnacle fan for life. The texture is chewy but the taste is surprisingly sweet and filled with the flavours of the ocean. These morsels are found deep in the intertidal zone or in areas with strong currents and in areas with surf-pounded rocks. The harvesting of these barnacles can be dangerous.

Mussel (*Mytilus* spp.) Mussels have a thin blue shell with waves of brown, purple, and black sometimes present. The peak time for mussels is in the fall, winter, and spring. Summer is the time for spawning and there are often elevated levels of biotoxins. The common wild blue mussel (*Mytilus edulis*) is abundant on rocks and shorelines all over Vancouver Island. Many commercial mussel farmers have selected the Mediterranean mussel (*Mytilus galloprovincialis*) and a new hybrid, the golden mussel (*Limnoperna fortunei*), for local cultivation.

Mussels can be gathered from rocks, outcrops, and ledges during low tide. They will often be linked together in clumps. Avoid pulling the string attaching the mussel to the rock. Avoid mussels that have been exposed to the air for long periods of time. Harvest as the tide is going out. Use mussels as soon as possible and keep refrigerated. Rinse the mussels in fresh water just before cooking to eliminate a little of the salt content.

Mussels do need a little more attention than most shellfish as they are somewhat more perishable. In a fresh mussel, the meat will be plump and sweet, filling the shell. As the mussel ages, it will feed on itself and wither in the shell. When a mussel dies, it starts to deteriorate quickly. Open shells are a sign of dead or dying mussels. You can try to close it to see if there is life still there, but if the shell springs back open, discard it. This is best to do before you cook the mussels. When cooking them, discard any mussels that do not open.

Oyster (*Crassostrea gigas*) The native oyster on this coast is the Olympia oyster (*Ostreola conchaphila*). The production is centred around the Puget Sound area but the oyster occurs sporadically all along the Pacific coast. Efforts are underway to restore the oyster on the coast. These efforts are being hampered by pollution, contamination, and predator concerns. This was the oyster that fed First Nations groups all along the coast.

Most of our local food oysters are variants on the Japanese oyster (*Crassostrea gigas*)

Shucking Oysters

An essential tool is the oyster-shucking knife. This is a thin and strong blade that is fairly dull. The trick to shucking oysters is to determine where the hinge of the oyster shell is. Hold the oyster with a kitchen towel (to prevent painful slips). Push the point of the knife into the hinge and give a quick flick of the wrist. This should pop open the shell. Once this happens, push in the knife and scrape it along the top of the shell to free the upper edge of the abductor muscle (which the oyster uses to clamp the shell tightly). The abductor muscle runs through the oyster and attaches the two halves of the shell. Once you have popped open the shell, run the knife under the oyster to release the bottom abductor muscle. Remove the oyster from the shell. Check for any pieces of shell that might be stuck to the meat and remove. It is good form to flip the oyster over to display the bottom. Discard any oysters that appear really dry. Place the oysters on ice and serve immediately.

You will find the larger the oyster, the stronger (and tougher) the shell. This also means that small oysters can be delicate and require more finesse rather than brute strength to open. It takes a little practice to master the art of shucking. Be sure to keep a firm grip on the oyster and after a few attempts you should be able to master the technique. It is important to keep the oysters chilled; serving them on ice will keep them cold and delicious as they are delivered to the table.

Large beach oysters are highly variable in size. If you have medium-large oysters, you'll need around 24 oysters to yield 1 pound of shucked meat. You can freeze shucked oysters by covering them with salted water (1 tsp [5 mL] salt per 1 cup [250 mL] water).

that has been cultivated in our waters since the early 1900s. The oyster rapidly spread and naturalized all along our coastline. The beach oysters are found in quiet bays, intertidal zones, and estuaries throughout the lower Pacific Northwest. Past the upper tip of Vancouver Island, the waters appear to be too cold for this introduced species.

Oysters are best harvested in the colder months; in the summer, they are spawning and appear and taste milky. There is a thriving aquaculture industry based on tray-farmed and beach-raised oysters.

8) Crustaceans

These beautiful creatures include crabs, prawns, and barnacles. They inhabit the intertidal zones of the coast. All of these organisms are members of the arthropod group of

Crab Preparation

For crab dishes with the best results, use fresh live crab. Once the crab is dead, the meat starts to break down and the fats darken, imparting bitter flavours to the meat. When purchasing crabs, beware that those that have been left a long time in the tank will slowly consume their own reserves of fat and then flesh. Only buy crab that is active and obviously still kicking. The fresher the better!

Boiling water will quickly kill the crab and is considered a fairly humane approach to dispatching the crab. Alternatively, you can plunge a sharp knife into the middle of the underside of the crab and push the back of the knife toward the head of the crab, splitting the shell. Another more gentle method is to put the crab in the freezer until it dies of hypothermia, about 10–15 minutes.

To cook a 1½ to 2 pound (about 680–900 kg) crab, bring a large stockpot of salted water to a boil. (The water can be flavoured with herbs, ginger, onions, celery, etc.) Add the whole crab and cook for about 8 minutes. If the water boils too rapidly and foams, reduce the heat to medium-high. Remove the crab with a pair of large tongs (or strain into a colander). Run cool water over the crab to stop the cooking process.

When cool enough to handle, take the crab and flip it on its back. Near the back end of the crab, you will see a small flap of shell called the apron. Using a spoon, lift the flap and remove. Holding the crab over the sink or bowl, grab the top shell near the back end and pull upward to separate the shell from the body. There will be a lot of juice and fat released (which can be reserved to add to a sauce). Using the spoon, remove the feather gills and guts of the crab and discard.

Run the crab quickly under water to remove any bits clinging to the meat. You can also use the spoon to remove any white cartilage covering the meat. At this point you can cut up the crab in between each leg if using the crab for stir-fries or if you will remove the meat as you eat.

To clean the meat, take the cut-up crab sections and remove the flesh with your fingers—a small fork or chopstick is a helpful tool. Try to keep the meat in as large of chunks as possible. Crack each leg or claw with the back of a chef's knife and break in half. Remove the meat with the chopstick or fork. Repeat with remaining crab. When finished, wash your hands and gently sift through the crab meat to feel for any pieces of shell that may have slipped through. Place the crab meat in a container with an airtight lid. A good trick is to place a piece of plastic wrap overtop of the meat, then seal with the lid. Save the shells to make crab bisque.

The crab meat is fairly fragile. Oxygen will start to blacken to the meat and turn the sweet flesh bitter. Commercially picked crab meat is usually frozen for safety and longevity. It is defrosted before it is sold. You will pay about 4 to 5 times the price per pound for crab meat as opposed to cooking a fresh crab—and you'll miss all the fun.

organisms and most have an exterior skeleton. They are subject to some fishing pressure due to their value as a food source and commercial harvesting activities.

Dungeness Crab (*Metacarcinus magister*) Dungeness crabs are some of the finest crabs in the world. They are voracious feeders in the intertidal zone and feed on a wide variety of prey including shellfish, octopus, and fish. The crabs are quite robust in the wild and have powerful pincers on their front two legs.

While a male Dungeness crab can grow to a shell width of 9 inches (23 cm), the minimum size limit for harvest in British Columbia is 6.5 inches (16.5 cm) across the maximum breadth of the shell. Most Dungeness crabs weigh between 1.5 pounds (680 g) and 3 pounds (1.4 kg). Dungeness crab is harvested in all months of the year.

Only male crabs are harvested and must be taken with baited traps but the fishery is relatively easy for anyone to start up and the crab is a relatively abundant and considered a sustainable resource. The crab prefers areas with sandy bottoms in water 30 to 150 feet (9–45 m) deep. Crabs like to hang out in bays, estuaries, inlets, and tidal streams.

Crabs from populated or industrial areas can store toxins and environmental pollutants. These often accumulate in the fatty tissue under the carapace shell. To minimize the presence of these toxins, it is advisable to clean the crab of top shell, gills, and fat before cooking.

Spot Prawn (*Pandalus platyceros*) There are seven commercial species of shrimp found in Canada's west coast waters. All cold-water shrimp are fast growing, short-lived, and have a high reproductive capacity, making these species less vulnerable to fishing pressure. The spot prawn is the largest of the species and is considered one of the best prawns in the world.

Spot prawns are caught in baited traps similar to crab traps. The commercial season generally lasts from early May to mid-June. It is good practice to throw back any small prawns, female prawns with eggs, and any bycatch species you may trap by accident. The other common shrimps include the side-stripe shrimp (*Pandalopsis dispar*) and pink shrimp (*Pandalus eous*).

REC

IPES

WILD PRESERVES

PANTRY

8 cups (2 L) stinging nettle tips
1 tsp (5 mL) vitamin C (such as Bernardin Fruit Fresh canning powder) (optional)
½ cup (125 mL) extra-virgin olive oil
1 tsp (5 mL) sea salt
1 tsp (5 mL) hot sauce

MAKES ABOUT 2 CUPS (500 ML)

STINGING NETTLE PESTO

Use gloves to collect the nettles and take only the top tips of the plant. Pick before the plant has flowered. Blanched nettles can be frozen for up to 2 months; vacuum pack for even longer storage life in the freezer.

Soak the stinging nettle tips in plenty of cold water. Rinse and drain. Bring a large pot of salted water (16 cups [4 L]) to a boil over high heat. Add the nettles and cook for 30 seconds, or until the nettles are limp and dark green. Remove the nettles from the pot with a slotted spoon or tongs and transfer to a large bowl of cold water. Shock (chill) the nettles to stop the cooking process. Drain the nettles and squeeze out all moisture. You will end up with a softball-sized lump of nettles.

In a food processor (or using mortar and pestle if you go old school), add the drained nettles and pulse to chop up. Purée to a paste, adding the vitamin C (if using) and then the oil in a slow and steady stream. You should have a smooth paste at this point. Season with salt and hot sauce to taste. Purée until smoothly mixed. Transfer to a storage container to refrigerate for 1 week, or freeze for up to 3 months.

Wild Greens Variations:
8 cups (2 L) oxeye daisy leaves and unopened buds
8 cups (2 L) miner's lettuce leaves and stems
8 cups (2 L) lamb's quarters leaves and stems
2 cups (500 mL) wild onions

Pesto

Making a pesto is a great way to preserve a bountiful harvest of wild herbs and plants. Pesto is an Italian technique that has its root in the word *pestare* (to pound or grind). Ancient Romans ground cheese, garlic, and herbs into a paste called *moretum*. In the more modern age, this commonly took the form of basil puréed with pine nuts, garlic, and cheese (the classic Pesto Genovese). Modern chefs take it to mean any purée of herbs or plants mixed with oil and seasoning. For a nuttier pesto, you can add 2 cups (500 mL) of roasted hazelnuts or sunflower seeds to the mix. You may have to add a little extra oil to make a smooth and soft pesto. Here are several wonderful variations based on foraged foods.

2 Tbsp (30 mL) grapeseed oil
1 cup (250 mL) peeled and chopped onions
8 cups (2 L) wild mushrooms (can be a blend)
2 Tbsp (30 mL) chopped fresh garlic
2 Tbsp (30 mL) chopped fresh sage
2 Tbsp (30 mL) chopped fresh parsley
2 Tbsp (30 mL) chopped fresh rosemary
½ cup (125 mL) extra-virgin olive oil
1 tsp (5 mL) sea salt
1 tsp (5 mL) hot sauce

MAKES ABOUT 2 CUPS (500 ML)

MUSHROOM PESTO

Use clean wild or cultivated mushrooms. Very carefully trim the mushrooms of any dirt and rinse under cold running water. Drain well and use immediately. This recipe works with many mushrooms, most successfully with chanterelles and boletes.

Warm a frying pan over high heat and add the grapeseed oil. When very hot, add the onions and sauté until they begin to soften. Add the mushrooms and season with salt and pepper. The mushrooms should immediately release moisture. Add the garlic, sage, parsley, and rosemary to the pan. Sauté until all the moisture is evaporated and the mushrooms begin to stick to the bottom of the pan. Transfer to a bowl and allow to cool slightly.

In a food processor, add the mushroom mixture and pulse to chop up. Purée to a paste, adding the olive oil in a slow and steady stream. You should have a smooth paste at this point. Season with salt and hot sauce to taste. Purée until smoothly mixed. Transfer to a storage container to refrigerate for 1 week, or freeze for up to 3 months.

4 cups (1 L) chopped seaweed leaves
1 cup (250 mL) toasted sunflower seeds
1 Tbsp (15 mL) chopped garlic
½ cup (125 mL) grapeseed oil
2 Tbsp (30 mL) light miso paste
1 tsp (5 mL) sea salt
1 tsp (5 mL) hot sauce

MAKES ABOUT 2 CUPS (500 ML)

SEAWEED PESTO

You can make this pesto equally well with fresh seaweed or dried seaweed that you have reconstituted. Simply soak the dried seaweed in cold water to refresh before using. My favourite seaweeds for this pesto are the softer varieties of laver (nori).

Heat a stockpot of water over high heat. Add the seaweed and cook for 1 minute, or until the seaweed softens. Drain and allow to cool slightly.

In a food processor, add the seaweed, sunflower seeds, and garlic. Pulse to chop up. Purée to a paste, adding the oil in a slow and steady stream. You should have a smooth paste at this point. Season to taste with miso, salt, and hot sauce. Purée until smoothly mixed. Transfer to a storage container to refrigerate for 1 week, or freeze for up to 3 months.

6 cups (1.5 L) blueberries, washed and rinsed
2 Tbsp (30 mL) lemon juice
4 cups (1 L) granulated sugar
1 tsp (5 mL) butter
2 pouches (170 mL) liquid pectin (such as Bernardin)

MAKES ABOUT 4 CUPS (1 L)

BLUEBERRY JAM

This is the basic technique for making most types of jam. Sugar is a great preservative and is needed for the proper set and for creating jam that is safe to use months down the road. It is important to use the quantities of sugar indicated. If you do not, keep the jam refrigerated or frozen until use. These recipes use a little less sugar than traditional recipes due to the use of liquid pectin as a thickening agent. Do not substitute powdered pectin for these recipes.

Heat a large, deep stainless steel saucepan over medium and add the blueberries. Crush with a potato masher. Stir in the lemon juice, sugar, and butter. Bring to a boil. Add the pectin and return to a boil for 1 minute, stirring constantly. Remove from the heat and skim off any foam.

Ladle the hot jam into a hot jar to within ¼ inch (0.6 cm) of the top of the jar. Tap the jar to remove any air bubbles. Wipe the jar rim to remove any jam residue. Place a lid on the clean jar rim. Screw the band down until resistance is met, then increase to gently tighten. Return the filled jar to the rack in the canner. Repeat for remaining jam.

When all the jam is used up and the jars are in the canner, make sure the jars are covered by at least 1 inch (2.5 cm) of water. Cover the canner and bring the water to a full, rolling boil, processing for a full 10 minutes. Turn the stove off, remove the canner lid, wait 5 minutes, then remove the jars without tilting, and place them upright on a cooling rack. Cool upright, undisturbed for at least a day.

Check each jar for a good seal. Sealed discs curve downward and do not move when pressed. Remove the screw bands; wipe and dry the bands and jars. Store the screw bands separately or replace loosely on the jars, as desired. Label and store the jars in a cool, dark place. For best quality, use the jam within 1 year. Any jars that have not sealed properly should be stored in the refrigerator.

Fruit Variations:

Use the same measurements of lemon juice, sugar, butter, and pectin as indicated above unless other variations are specified.

6 cups (1.5 L) strawberries

6 cups (1.5 L) blackberries (crush the fruit and add an equal amount of sugar; use only 1 pouch of pectin)

6 cups (1.5 L) huckleberries (crush the fruit and add an equal amount of sugar; use only 1 pouch of pectin)

8 cups (2 L) salal berries (use 1 cup water and 4 cups sugar; omit the pectin)

For Jellies:

3 cups (750 mL) Oregon grape juice (use 2 cups sugar and only 1 pouch of pectin; omit the lemon juice)

6 cups (1.5 L) water
12 cups (3 L) rosehips, washed and trimmed
4 cups (1 L) granulated sugar
juice of 1 lemon
2 pouches (170 mL) liquid pectin (such as Bernardin)

MAKES ABOUT 6 CUPS (1.5 L)

ROSEHIP BUTTER

In the Pacific Northwest, wild Nootka roses (and several other wild roses) produce prolific amounts of rose hips. Pick the hips in late fall, once the evenings become cool. A touch of frost is even good for developing the best flavour of the butter.

Heat a heavy-bottomed saucepan over medium-high. Add the water and rosehips and bring to a simmer. Cook for about 10 minutes to soften the rosehips. Purée with an immersion blender or process in batches in a blender.

Using a fine strainer, strain the juice from the purée into a bowl. Press the purée with the back of a ladle or spoon to extract all the juice from the rosehips. Measure the juice; you should have about 4 cups (1 L). Add juice to a clean heavy-bottomed saucepan and add an equal amount of sugar. Bring to a boil and add the lemon juice and pectin. Return to a boil, then remove from the heat, and skim off any foam.

Ladle the hot liquid into a hot jar to within ¼ inch (0.6 cm) of top of the jar. Tap the jar to remove any air bubbles. Wipe the jar rim, removing any residue. Place a lid on the clean jar rim. Screw the band down until resistance is met, then increase to gently tighten. Return the filled jar to the rack in the canner. Repeat for remaining rosehip mixture.

When all the liquid is used up and the jars are in the canner, make sure the jars are covered by at least 1 inch (2.5 cm) of water. Cover the canner and bring the water to a full, rolling boil, processing for a full 10 minutes. Turn the stove off, remove the canner lid, wait 5 minutes, then remove the jars without tilting, and place them upright on a cooling rack. Cool upright, undisturbed for at least a day.

Check each jar for a good seal. Sealed discs curve downward and do not move when pressed. Remove the screw bands; wipe and dry the bands and jars. Store the screw bands separately or replace loosely on the jars, as desired. Label and store the jars in a cool, dark place. For best quality, use the rosehip butter within 1 year. Any jars that have not sealed properly should be stored in the refrigerator.

2 cups (500 mL) water
3 cups (750 mL) grand fir needles,
  washed and trimmed
1 cup (250 mL) sweet cicely leaves
  (or spinach leaves)

3 cups (750 mL) granulated sugar
juice of 1 lemon
2 pouches (170 mL) liquid pectin
  (such as Bernardin)

MAKES ABOUT 4 CUPS (1 L)

GRAND FIR JELLY

The needles of many coniferous trees are packed with nutrients and vitamin C. My favourite are the needles of the grand fir. It is important to remove the needles from the branches as the bark will contribute significant tannins to the jelly.

Heat a heavy-bottomed saucepan over medium-high. Add the water and bring to a boil. Add the fir needles and sweet cicely and remove from the heat. Allow to steep for 5 minutes.

Using a fine strainer, strain the juice from the mixture into a bowl. Swirl the mixture with the back of a ladle or spoon to extract all the juice from the needles. Measure the juice; you should have about 2 cups (500 mL). Add to a clean heavy-bottomed saucepan and add the sugar. Bring to a boil and add the lemon juice and pectin. Return to a boil, remove from the heat, and skim off any foam.

Ladle the hot jelly into a hot jar to within ¼ inch (0.6 cm) of top of jar. Tap the jar to remove any air bubbles. Wipe the jar rim, removing any jam residue. Place a lid on the clean jar rim. Screw the band down until resistance is met, then increase to gently tighten. Return the filled jar to the rack in the canner. Repeat for remaining jelly.

When all the jelly is used up and the jars are in the canner, make sure the jars are covered by at least 1 inch (2.5 cm) of water. Cover the canner and bring the water to a full, rolling boil, processing for a full 10 minutes. Turn the stove off, remove the canner lid, wait 5 minutes, then remove the jars without tilting, and place them upright on a cooling rack. Cool upright, undisturbed for at least a day.

Check each jar for a good seal. Sealed discs curve downward and do not move when pressed. Remove the screw bands; wipe and dry the bands and jars. Store the screw bands separately or replace loosely on the jars, as desired. Label and store the jars in a cool, dark place. For best quality, use the jelly within 1 year. Any jars that have not sealed properly should be stored in the refrigerator.

Needle Variations:
3 cups (750 mL) Douglas fir
  needles
3 cups (750 mL) hemlock fir
  needles

3 cups (750 mL) spruce needles
3 cups (750 mL) pine needles
3 cups (750 mL) cedar tips

3½ cups (875 mL) water
2 cups (500 mL) lightly packed fresh mint leaves
½ cup (125 mL) white wine vinegar
2 pouches (170 mL) liquid pectin (such as Bernardin)
4 cups (1 L) granulated sugar

MAKES ABOUT 5 CUPS (1.25 L)

WILD MINT JELLY

Wild mint grows all over most of the temperate regions of the planet. Make sure the mint is picked from areas that are uncontaminated from pollution or animal feces. Rinse the mint thoroughly and soak in clean, cold water before processing. Wild mint has lots of essential oils and has a strong peppermint flavour. This is a vinegar-based jelly, traditionally used with roasted lamb or pork but excellent with strong cheeses like goat or blue cheese.

In a saucepan over high, heat the water. Add the mint and muddle with a wooden spoon. Let the mixture infuse for 15 minutes. Strain the liquid into a measuring cup; you should have about 3 cups (750 mL).

Heat a heavy-bottomed saucepan over medium-high and add the mint infusion, vinegar, and pectin. Bring to a boil and stir in the sugar. Return to a rolling boil for about 1 minute. Remove from the heat and skim off any foam that has formed.

Ladle the hot liquid into a hot jar to within ¼ inch (0.6 cm) of the top of the jar. Tap the jar to remove any air bubbles. Wipe the jar rim, removing any residue. Place a lid on the clean jar rim. Screw the band down until resistance is met, then increase to gently tighten. Return the filled jar to the rack in the canner. Repeat for remaining jelly.

When all the jelly is used up and the jars are in the canner, make sure the jars are covered by at least 1 inch (2.5 cm) of water. Cover the canner and bring the water to a full, rolling boil, processing for a full 10 minutes.

Turn the stove off, remove the canner lid, wait 5 minutes, then remove the jars without tilting, and place them upright on a cooling rack. Cool upright, undisturbed for at least a day.

Check each jar for a good seal. Sealed discs curve downward and do not move when pressed. Remove the screw bands; wipe and dry the bands and jars. Store the screw bands separately or replace loosely on the jars, as desired. Label and store the jars in a cool, dark place. For best quality, use the mint jelly within 1 year. Any jars that have not sealed properly should be stored in the refrigerator.

2 cups (500 mL) honey
2 cups (500 mL) grand fir needle shoots

MAKES ABOUT 2 CUPS (500 ML)

GRAND FIR–INFUSED HONEY

Grand fir needles were traditionally used by West Coast First Nations as a flavour agent for food and as a medicinal herb. Traditional firepit cooking used fir boughs to smoke and flavour a wide range of seafood and meats, including salmon. In the spring, honey can be infused with the new-growth shoots of fir, resulting in distinct flavours reminiscent of rosemary, lemon, and pine mingled in a pleasant sweet package.

Heat a heavy-bottomed saucepan over medium and add the honey. Warm until the liquid has thinned considerably, about 2–3 minutes. Add the grand fir needle shoots, stir to mix well, and remove from the heat. Allow to infuse for 15 minutes. Pour through a fine mesh strainer into a bowl or container. To store, transfer to a glass canning jar and seal with a lid. Cool to room temperature. The honey will keep for 4–6 months.

Variations:
2 cups (500 mL) Douglas fir shoots
2 cups (500 mL) hemlock fir shoots
2 cups (500 mL) spruce tips
2 cups (500 mL) pine needles
2 cups (500 mL) cedar tips

2 cups (500 mL) water
4 cups (1 L) white sugar
2 cups (500 mL) rose petals, packed

MAKES ABOUT 4 CUPS (1 L)

ROSE PETAL SYRUP

You can make wonderful syrups with any of the variety of products suggested in the grand fir–infused honey recipe (p. 83). In addition, the syrup can be used to capture the essence of more delicate and floral elements like wild rose petals. A good trick to extend the shelf life of the syrup is to add 1 tablespoon (15 mL) of alcohol, such as vodka or white rum to the hot syrup.

In a saucepan over medium, heat the water and add the sugar slowly. Bring to a boil, add the rose petals, and remove from the heat.

Allow the syrup to cool completely. Strain into a glass storage container and refrigerate until needed. It should keep for several months.

Variations:
2 cups (500 mL) wild herbs, such as mint, fennel, or sweet cicely
4 cups (1 L) whole ripe rosehips, cooked and puréed (blend cooked rosehips until smooth; add as you would rose petals; strain syrup to remove all pulp)

2 cups (500 mL) apple cider vinegar
2 cups (500 mL) apple cider
1 cup (250 mL) peeled and diced onion
1 cup (250 mL) peeled and diced carrot
1 cup (250 mL) diced celery
1 cup (250 mL) sugar
1 Tbsp (15 mL) sea salt
1 Tbsp (15 mL) pickling spice
1 Tbsp (15 mL) grainy mustard
2 Tbsp (30 mL) chopped garlic
1 Tbsp (15 mL) minced ginger
2 Tbsp (30 mL) chopped fresh sage
4 cups (1 L) peeled and diced burdock root
1 Tbsp (15 mL) tapioca starch (or cornstarch, mixed with equal parts cold water)

MAKES ABOUT 8 CUPS (2 L)

BURDOCK CHUTNEY

Burdock roots are long, thin taproots that can easily reach lengths of 10 inches (25 cm) or more. As you peel the roots, immediately place them in water with vinegar, lemon, or vitamin C (to prevent browning). Cut the burdock into a medium dice and then place back into the treated water. Strain just before using.

Heat a heavy-bottomed saucepan over medium-high. Add the cider vinegar, apple cider, onion, carrot, celery, sugar, salt, pickling spice, mustard, garlic, ginger, and sage. Bring to a boil and add the burdock root. Return to a boil, reduce the heat, and simmer for 10 minutes or until burdock is tender. Add the tapioca starch and stir until the mixture thickens.

Ladle the chutney into two 1-quart (1 L) canning jars. Tap the jars to remove any air bubbles. Wipe the jar rims, removing any residue. Place lids on clean jar rims. Screw bands down until resistance is met, then increase to gently tighten. Cool jars upright, undisturbed until cool to the touch.

Label jars and store in the refrigerator for at least 1 week before opening.

4 cups (1 L) pickling vinegar
2 cups (500 mL) sugar
⅓ cup (75 mL) sea salt
2 Tbsp (30 mL) pickling spice
2 slices fresh ginger
1 stick cinnamon
4 cups (1 L) prepared cattail shoots (see recipe headnote)

MAKES ABOUT 4 CUPS (1 L)

PICKLED CATTAIL SHOOTS

Cattail shoots are found at the base of young cattails. The shoots should separate easily from the roots. Use the bottom whitish portion of the stalk. Peel off the outer layers until the solid white core is reached. Trim the core into 2-inch (5 cm) pieces. Soak well in cold water before using. I use a commercial brand of pickling spice (McCormick) with great results.

Heat a heavy-bottomed saucepan over medium-high. Add the pickling vinegar, sugar, sea salt, pickling spice, ginger, and cinnamon. Bring to a boil and add the cattail shoots. Return to a boil and simmer for 5 minutes.

Spoon the cattails into a 1-quart (1 L) canning jar. Ladle hot pickling brine to within ¼ inch (0.6 cm) of the top of the jar. Tap the jar to remove any air bubbles. Wipe the jar rim, removing any residue. Place a lid on the clean jar rim. Screw the band down until resistance is met, then increase to gently tighten. Cool upright, undisturbed until cool to the touch.

Label the jar and store in the refrigerator for at least 1 week before opening.

APPETIZERS

5½ cups (1.375 L) all-purpose flour
2 tsp (10 mL) salt
1 lb (454 g) lard or shortening
1 egg
1 Tbsp (15 mL) vinegar

MAKES 4 PORTIONS, OR ENOUGH DOUGH FOR
4 SINGLE-CRUST 10-INCH (25 CM) PIES

BASIC FLAKY PIE DOUGH

A versatile pie dough that works well for desserts or savoury pies. Mixing gently to bring the dough just together makes a very tender and flaky pastry. Freeze any leftover dough for up to 1 month.

In a mixing bowl, stir together the flour and salt. Cut the lard or shortening into rough cubes and toss in the flour. Cut in the lard using a pastry cutter or two knives until the mixture resembles pea-sized lumps. In a measuring cup, beat the egg with a fork. Add the vinegar and enough cold water to make 1 cup (250 mL). Stir the liquid into the flour mixture until incorporated and the dough starts to come together. Gently knead until the mixture just comes together in a ball. Divide the dough into 4 portions. Cover each one with plastic wrap and refrigerate for at least 1 hour.

When ready to proceed, roll out the dough on a floured work surface, using a good dusting of flour on the dough and rolling pin. Proceed with the directions in the pie recipe. The dough can also be frozen for up to 1 month.

2 medium leeks, trimmed and washed

6 slices bacon, cut into thick strips (optional—see Chef's Tip)

1 Tbsp (15 mL) minced fresh garlic

8 cups (2 L) wild greens (nettles, lamb's quarters, miner's lettuce, etc.)

¼ cup (60 mL) white wine

1 portion (¼ of recipe) basic flaky pie dough (p. 90)

2 cups (500 mL) cream (or half-and-half)

4 eggs

1 Tbsp (15 mL) minced fresh thyme

salt and pepper, to taste

SERVES 6–8

WEED PIE (WILD GREENS QUICHE)

This is a great pie for the springtime when all the fresh greens are available. I love this with stinging nettles and many other springtime greens. This tart is particularly good with blanched stinging nettles but many wild greens work well.

Cut the leeks into thin strips, using only the white and light green parts. Heat a skillet over medium-high. Add the bacon and cook until it begins to brown and renders fat. Pour off most of the fat and discard. Add the leeks, garlic, and greens; stir until they begin to soften and brown. Add the white wine and cook until the mixture is completely evaporated. Season well with salt and pepper. Allow to cool to room temperature.

Roll out the chilled, rested dough on a well-floured surface. Place the dough into a pie tin, preferably one with a removable metal bottom and a fluted edge. Keep the dough very slack around the edge of the pie tin. Chill the dough for at least 15 minutes. Once the dough is chilled, preheat the oven to 350°F (180°C). Place a sheet of aluminum foil in the tin and roll the edges so the foil sheet fits snugly in the tin. Bake the crust in the oven for 15 minutes.

Meanwhile in a mixing bowl, add the greens and leek mixture. Pour in the cream and add the eggs. Whisk until mixed. Add the thyme and season well with salt and pepper. Pour the mixture into the hot pie shell, place the pie on a tray, and return it to the oven. Cook for 40 minutes or until the tart filling is browned and starts to puff slightly. Remove from the oven and place on a cooling rack. Serve warm, or chill and reheat before serving.

Chef's Tip: For a vegetarian quiche, substitute 1 Tbsp (15 mL) olive oil for the bacon.

1 Tbsp (15 mL) grapeseed oil

1 small onion, chopped

2 cups (500 mL) chopped chanterelle mushrooms

1 lb (454 g) ground beef

1 Tbsp (15 mL) sea salt

1 Tbsp (15 mL) chopped garlic

1 Tbsp (15 mL) chopped fresh thyme leaves

1 small potato, peeled and finely diced

1 medium carrot, peeled and finely diced

1 cup (250 mL) beer (or beef stock or water)

1 Tbsp (15 mL) hot sauce

1 Tbsp (15 mL) mild curry paste (or powder)

½ cup (125 mL) breadcrumbs

1 full recipe basic flaky pie dough (p. 90)

1 egg, beaten

MAKES 24 TURNOVERS

CURRIED BEEF AND CHANTERELLE MUSHROOM TURNOVERS

This recipe is reminiscent of Jamaican pasties, which often feature a bright yellow crust. If you want this effect, add 1 tablespoon (15 mL) of turmeric to the flour of the basic flaky pie dough (p. 90) and proceed with the recipe. The pastries can be made in advance and frozen. These turnovers are great served with burdock chutney (p. 86).

Warm a large skillet over medium-high heat and add the oil and onion. Sauté until the onion begins to soften and slightly brown. Add the chanterelles and sauté until they release moisture and begin to stick to the bottom of the pan. Add the beef and season with salt. Sauté until the beef is browned and crumbling, about 5 minutes.

Add the garlic, thyme, potato, and carrot. Sauté until the mixture again begins to stick to the bottom of the pot. Add the beer and stir to dissolve the brown bits at the bottom of the pan. Reduce the heat to a simmer and cook until the potato and carrot are tender. Season with hot sauce and curry paste. Add enough breadcrumbs to absorb most of the moisture left in the pan. The mixture should appear only slightly moist. Remove from the heat and allow to cool.

WHITE AND YELLOW CHANTERELLES

Preheat the oven to 400°F (200°C).

On a well-floured surface, take a small golf ball of dough and flatten it with your palm. Dust it with more flour and roll out into a 6-inch (15 cm) circle using a rolling pin. Place about ¼ cup (60 mL) of beef filling in the centre of the pastry, spread it into a log across the diameter, leaving a 1-inch (2.5 cm) border along the edges. Brush the edges of the pastry with the egg wash using a pastry brush. Fold over the dough to make a half moon shape, enclosing the filling. Press with a fork or pinch with your fingers to make a nice seal. Place on a baking tray and brush the top with additional egg wash. Repeat with remaining dough and filling.

Bake the turnovers for about 15–20 minutes, or until golden brown. Serve warm.

4 cups (1 L) stinging nettle tips
2 cups (500 mL) cooked chickpeas
1 Tbsp (15 mL) chopped fresh garlic
zest and juice of 1 lemon
¼ cup (60 mL) extra-virgin olive oil
1 tsp (5 mL) hot sauce
salt and pepper, to taste

SERVES 6–8

STINGING NETTLE HUMMUS

Chickpeas are a versatile platform for the flavour of many wild foods. Greens, mushrooms, and seaweed all work well in this mixture. Some greens of note are miner's lettuce, oxeye daisy leaves, and wild mustard greens.

Soak the stinging nettles in plenty of cold water. Rinse and drain them. Bring a large pot of salted water to boil over high heat. Add the nettles and cook for 30 seconds or until the nettles are limp and dark green. Remove with a slotted spoon or tongs and transfer to a large bowl of cold water. When cool, drain the nettles and squeeze out all moisture. You will end up with a small ball of nettles. Coarsely chop the nettles.

In a food processor, purée the nettles and chickpeas until a coarse mixture forms. Add the garlic, lemon zest, and lemon juice. Continue to purée the mixture, adding the olive oil in a slow stream until the mixture is very smooth. Add the hot sauce and season well with salt and pepper. Pulse to mix, then transfer to a serving dish, drizzle with a little more olive oil, and serve with rustic bread or pita bread.

8 cups (2 L) stinging nettles
1 Tbsp (15 mL) extra-virgin olive oil
salt and pepper, to taste
8 sheets phyllo pastry
2 Tbsp (30 mL) extra-virgin olive oil (or hazelnut oil), for brushing on pastry
¼ cup (60 mL) hazelnuts, finely chopped
1 package (7 oz [200 g]) fresh mozzarella

MAKES 8 ROLLS

CRISPY STINGING NETTLE AND MOZZARELLA ROLLS

This dish is best with fresh mozzarella, often marketed as bocconcini or a richer variety made with cream called burrata cheese.

Preheat the oven to 375°F (190°F).

Bring a pot of salted water to boil and add the nettles. Cook for 1 minute, then transfer to a bowl of cold water. When cool, drain the water. Take the drained nettles and squeeze into a ball. With a chef's knife, chop the ball into slices and chop the slices into a rough dice. Transfer into a bowl, drizzle with olive oil, and season with salt and pepper.

Place a phyllo sheet on a clean work surface. Brush it with olive oil and sprinkle one half with an eighth of the chopped hazelnuts. Fold the sheet over to make a long, narrow rectangle. Lay a thin line of chopped nettles along the left (short) side of the sheet. Cut the mozzarella into slices and cut each slice into strips. Lay a few strips of cheese over the nettles to cover.

Working from the left, fold the phyllo overtop of the filling. Compress the filling to make a tight log. Roll the filling a couple of times in phyllo until a very tight log is formed. Fold over the top and bottom edges of the phyllo sheet to seal in the ends of the log. Continue rolling the filling into a tight roll. When you get to the end of the sheet, brush the edge with a little oil and fold to seal tightly. Place on a tray covered with parchment (or silicone) paper and refrigerate until needed. Repeat with remaining filling and phyllo.

Brush chilled rolls with a little olive oil and place in the oven. Bake for 10–12 minutes, or until the pastry is browned and crisp. Transfer to serving plates and serve warm.

4 cups (1 L) burdock root, scrubbed and peeled
1 carrot, peeled and julienned (optional)
1 Tbsp (15 mL) minced garlic
3 Tbsp (45 mL) light soy sauce
2 tsp (10 mL) mirin
1 tsp (5 mL) sesame oil
1 tsp (5 mL) hot sauce (or chili paste)

MAKES 4 CUPS

BURDOCK ROOT (GOBO) SNACK

The roots of the burdock family are a favourite treat in Asian countries, particularly in Japan where they are featured as an appetizer or snack while drinking beer. The root is astringent when raw but transforms into a delicious and chewy treat once cooked. Kind of like a vegan version of beef jerky!

Julienne the burdock root into thin strips or shave with a vegetable peeler. Place shredded burdock in cold water and soak for 30 minutes, then drain (this helps remove a little of the astringency from the roots).

In a saucepan over medium heat, add the burdock, carrot (if using), and garlic. Cook for 4–5 minutes. Add the soy sauce, mirin, sesame oil, and hot sauce. Simmer for an additional 10 minutes or until the burdock is slightly tender (will still have a bite to it). Remove from the heat, allow to cool, and refrigerate until needed. Will store for up to 2 weeks.

1 cup (250 mL) oxeye daisy leaves
¼ cup (60 mL) white wine
2 cups (500 mL) thick Greek or Balkan-style yogurt
1 tsp (5 mL) honey
juice and zest of 1 lemon
¼ cup (60 mL) whipping cream

MAKES ABOUT 2 CUPS (500 ML)

PRESSED YOGURT WITH OXEYE DAISY PURÉE

The creamy consistency of thickened yogurt is a nice foil for the earthy green flavours of wild plants. People are always surprised at how wonderful this tastes. I sometimes use the yogurt as a base for bigleaf maple syrup or infused syrups with similarly excellent and sweeter results.

In a food processor, add the oxeye daisy leaves. Purée until smooth, scraping down the sides occasionally. Add the wine and purée until very smooth. Refrigerate until needed.

In a small bowl, combine the yogurt, honey, lemon juice and zest, and whipping cream. Whisk to mix and let sit for 15 minutes.

Line a wire mesh sieve with paper towels or cheesecloth. Add the yogurt mixture and place over a bowl. Fold cheesecloth overtop of the yogurt and place a small plate on top. Place in the refrigerator and allow to sit for at least 2 hours, or until the yogurt thickens and the bowl has accumulated a cloudy liquid. Remove the yogurt from the sieve and transfer to a storage container.

To serve, spread the yogurt on a serving plate. Top with the purée of oxeye daisy leaves and serve immediately with fresh bread for dipping. Also great as a base for a salad plate with roasted beets or smoked salmon.

2 Tbsp (30 mL) butter
½ cup (125 mL) finely chopped wild onions
2 Tbsp (30 mL) flour
1 tsp (5 mL) French's mustard powder (or 1 Tbsp [15 mL] prepared mustard)
1 cup (250 mL) milk
½ cup (125 mL) apple cider (or beer)
1 tsp (5 mL) Worcestershire sauce
½ cup (125 mL) blue cheese (like Stilton)
½ cup (125 mL) aged white cheddar cheese
salt and pepper, to taste
4 slices good rustic bread
additional chopped wild onions, for garnish

SERVES 4

WELSH RAREBIT WITH WILD ONIONS

This is a dish from my culinary heritage in Wales. It really is a fancy version of cheese on toast. It is also great with fresh leeks. When you make it with good-quality cheese, it is truly a work of art. This is one of the treats I always make with the first crop of wild onions. It has become something of a ritual and a celebration of a rare and precious wild product returning to us each spring.

Preheat the oven to broil.

In a saucepan over medium-high heat, melt the butter. Add the wild onions and sauté for 1–2 minutes. Add the flour and mustard powder and whisk until a smooth paste is formed. Add the milk, cider, and Worcestershire sauce. Whisk until the sauce thickens. Reduce the heat to low and cook for 5 minutes, stirring occasionally.

Grate the cheeses. Add to the sauce and stir until melted and the sauce has thickened. Taste and adjust seasoning with salt and pepper if necessary. Remove from the heat and allow to cool. Toast the bread lightly and place on a baking tray, top with the cooled sauce, making an even thick layer. Sprinkle with the additional raw wild onions. Place under the broiler and cook until the sauce begins to brown and the onions slightly char, about 3–4 minutes. Serve immediately. Reserve any extra sauce; it makes a great topping for tuna or salmon melts.

8 cups (2 L) wild greens (lamb's quarters, oxeye daisy, dandelion, mustard, etc.)
1 tsp (5 mL) extra-virgin olive oil
4 slices bacon, minced
1 Tbsp (15 mL) minced garlic
¼ cup (60 mL) white wine (or water)
1 Tbsp (15 mL) soy sauce
1 tsp (5 mL) honey
½ tsp (2 mL) ground black pepper

SERVES 4

WILD GREENS SAUTÉED WITH GARLIC, BACON, AND SOY

Many greens are great when sautéed with bacon. In fact one of the common European names for lamb's quarters translates to "bacon greens." Like many of the dishes in this book, the meat component is optional and meant for flavour but is not a significant part of the dish. It is excellent without it. But if you don't mind—try the bacon!

Soak the greens in lots of cold water and trim off any thick stems or damaged leaves. Heat a skillet over medium-high and add the olive oil and minced bacon. Sauté to cook the bacon and render off the fat. Pour off about half the fat.

Add the greens and garlic to the pan and toss to coat. Add the white wine and reduce until the liquid is almost evaporated. Add the soy sauce, honey, and pepper. Toss to coat. Taste and adjust with salt if necessary (this depends on how salty your soy sauce is—I use low sodium versions).

Transfer to a serving platter and serve warm.

BREADS & SAVOURIES

1 Tbsp (15 mL) instant yeast
2 cups (500 mL) warm water, divided
1 tsp (5 mL) honey
3 cups (750 mL) multigrain bread flour
1 cup (250 mL) all-purpose flour
2 Tbsp (30 mL) porcini powder (p. 19)
1 Tbsp (15 mL) chopped fresh rosemary
1 tsp (5 mL) salt

SERVES 4–6

GRILLED MULTIGRAIN MUSHROOM FLATBREAD

This bread is a staple at my place. I make the dough the night before and let it rise gently in the refrigerator. The trick of cooking it on the grill always seems to amaze people. It is often served with hummus (p. 96) made with mushrooms, stinging nettles, or other wild greens blended in with the chickpeas.

In a small measuring cup, combine the yeast, 1 cup (250 mL) of the warm water, and the honey. Allow to sit for 5 minutes to bloom the yeast.

In the bowl of a mixer fitted with a dough hook, add the bread flour, all-purpose flour, porcini powder, rosemary, and salt. Add the yeast mixture and process on medium speed. Clean the sides of the bowl with a spatula to mix in the flour. With the machine running, add half of the remaining warm water to the bowl and keep processing. If the mixture appears dry, keep adding water until a soft and moist dough is formed. It will usually take all of the water to make this happen.

Transfer the moist dough to a floured surface and knead the dough until a smooth texture is developed. Transfer the dough to a large plastic bag (I use zip-lock bags) and place in the refrigerator overnight to proof.

The next day, remove the dough and place on a floured work surface. Divide the dough into 8 small balls. Flatten each ball with your hand and make a small, flat disc. Cover with a dry towel and let rest for 15 minutes. Clean the grill and preheat to high.

Place the dough discs onto the hot grill and cook for about 5 minutes or until the dough stiffens and the bottoms are an even golden brown. If the dough starts to scorch, flip the discs and turn down the heat. The bread will sound hollow when tapped when you are close to cooking through. Serve warm as soon as possible.

Focaccia

1 Tbsp (15 mL) instant yeast

2 cups (500 mL) warm water

1 tsp (5 mL) honey

6 cups (1.5 L) unbleached bread
flour

2 cups (500 mL) cold mashed
potatoes

1 tsp (5 mL) salt

Topping

4 Tbsp (60 mL) chopped fresh
grand fir needle tips

1 onion, peeled, trimmed, and
thinly sliced

1 cup (250 mL) extra-virgin olive oil

1 cup (250 mL) warm water

1 Tbsp (15 mL) coarse sea salt

MAKES 1 LARGE FLAT LOAF

POTATO FOCACCIA WITH ONIONS AND GRAND FIR NEEDLES

This is a traditional Italian bread made amazing by the addition of grand fir needles to the topping. Use the tips of the needles that are tender and brighter green. The olive oil and water mixture that is poured on top makes a crisp and chewy crust.

In a small measuring cup, combine the yeast, warm water, and honey. Allow to sit for 5 minutes to bloom the yeast.

In the bowl of a mixer fitted with a dough hook, add the flour, mashed potatoes, and salt. Add half the yeast mixture and process on medium speed. Clean the sides of the bowl with a spatula and keep adding the rest of the yeast mixture until a soft and moist dough is formed. Depending on the flour, it may not take all the mixture, or you may have to add some additional water.

Transfer the moist dough to a floured surface and knead the dough until a smooth texture is developed. Return the dough to the mixer bowl and cover with a clean kitchen cloth. Let the dough sit in a warm spot for about 1 hour. Transfer the dough to a floured cutting board, dust with flour, and roll out into a rectangle. Place on a roasting pan lined with parchment paper and spread out the dough to completely cover the sheet. Cover with the towel and let sit to rise a second time, about 1 hour.

Once the dough has risen, preheat the oven to 400°F (200°C). Push the dough with your fingers to dimple the entire surface of the dough. Sprinkle with grand fir needles and onion slices. Place olive oil and water in a small bottle and shake to form an emulsion. Pour over the dough and season well with coarse salt. Place in the oven. Bake for 25–30 minutes, or until the dough is golden brown and the onions are slightly charred.

2 cups (500 mL) all-purpose flour
3 Tbsp (45 mL) sugar
1 Tbsp (15 mL) baking powder
½ tsp (2 mL) baking soda
1 tsp (5 mL) sea salt
¼ cup (60 mL) shredded rose petals
½ cup (125 mL) chilled butter
¾ cup (175 mL) buttermilk (or cream)
1 egg

MAKES 8 LARGE SCONES

WILD ROSE PETAL SCONES

The best scones are light and fluffy with a crisp crust and a tender centre. The secret is gentle handling of the dough and keeping all the ingredients cold before mixing. This allows the butter to keep its shape before baking, melting into tender, flaky layers. These scones are also excellent with dried wild berries, fir needle tips (springtime only), and dried seaweed flakes. The rose scones are amazing with any homemade jam or jelly.

In a large mixing bowl, combine the flour, sugar, baking powder, baking soda, sea salt, and rose petals. Stir to mix. Cut the chilled butter into small cubes and add to the flour. Toss with flour to coat. Using a pastry cutter (or two butter knives), chop the butter into fine pieces the size of peas.

In a small bowl, add the buttermilk and egg. Whisk with a fork until blended. Add the buttermilk and egg mixture to the dough and fold with a spatula to distribute the liquid. Gently bring the dough together with your hands until a moist dough ball is formed. Place in the refrigerator and chill for at least 30 minutes.

Preheat the oven to 350°F (180°C).

Return the dough to a floured board, sprinkle with flour, and form into a round, flat shape. Use your hands to bring any scraps into the dough and smooth the sides. With a knife or pastry cutter, divide the round into 8 wedges. Transfer to a baking tray lined with silicone or parchment paper. Place in the oven and bake for 15–20 minutes, or until golden brown.

Transfer to a cooling rack. Can be eaten as is or glazed with a topping of icing sugar moistened with a little cream or buttermilk.

1 Tbsp (15 mL) instant yeast
1 cup (250 mL) warm milk (see Chef's Tip)
1 tsp (5 mL) honey
4 cups (1 L) all-purpose flour
1 tsp (5 mL) salt
2 Tbsp (30 mL) melted butter

1 cup (250 mL) water
1 cup (250 mL) dried or fresh berries (blueberry, huckleberry, cranberry, etc.)
2 Tbsp (30 mL) grapeseed oil, plus more for each batch

MAKES 8–12 BANNOCK

WILD BERRY BANNOCK

I make a yeast bannock that has a soft springy texture when freshly pan-fried. I use a kitchen mixer with a dough hook to process the dough. If you do not have this tool, use a bowl and wooden spoon to get the mixture started, then knead to a smooth consistency with your hands. Traditionally, this dough is fried in oil or lard, but I like the results of using a little oil in a non-stick or cast-iron pan.

In a small measuring cup, combine the yeast, warm milk, and honey. Allow to sit for 5 minutes to bloom the yeast.

In the bowl of a mixer fitted with a dough hook, add the flour and salt. Add the milk and yeast mixture and the butter. Process on medium speed. Clean the sides of the bowl with a spatula to mix in the flour. With the machine running, add half of the water to the bowl and keep processing. If the mixture appears dry, keep adding water until a soft and moist dough is formed. It will usually take all of the water to make this happen.

Transfer the moist dough to a floured surface. Sprinkle with the dried fruit and knead into the dough until a smooth texture is developed. Transfer the dough to a large plastic bag (I use zip-lock bags) and place in the refrigerator overnight to proof.

The next day, remove the dough and place on a floured work surface. Divide the dough into 8 medium balls or 12 small balls. Flatten each ball with your hand and make a small, flat disc. Cover with a dry towel and let rest for 10 minutes.

Preheat the oven to warm.

Heat a skillet over medium and add the oil. Pan-fry the dough in batches, about 5 minutes per side. If the dough starts to scorch, flip the dough and turn down the heat. The bannock will sound hollow when tapped when you are close to cooking through. Add more oil for subsequent batches. Transfer to a warm oven and repeat with the remaining dough. Serve warm as soon as possible.

Chef's Tip: To warm the milk, you can microwave it for 1 minute. It should only be hot enough that you can still dip your finger in the liquid without burning yourself (about 110°F [45°C]).

4 large potatoes, peeled (about 2 lb [about 1 kg])
1 cup (250 mL) wild onions (or green onions), trimmed and thinly sliced
1 egg, lightly beaten
¼ cup (60 mL) all-purpose flour
¾ tsp (4 mL) salt
½ tsp (2 mL) baking powder
¼ tsp (1 mL) pepper
2 Tbsp (30 mL) vegetable oil

SERVES 4–6

POTATO AND WILD ONION LATKES

A latke is a potato pancake that is excellent as a foil for smoked salmon or great with any type of egg preparation for breakfast. I also like to add wild greens like miner's lettuce, purslane, and young dandelion leaves to the batter for a nice herbal quality.

Using a coarse grater, shred the potatoes and place in a large colander or sieve; squeeze or press out as much liquid as possible and discard. In large bowl, stir together the potato, onions, egg, flour, salt, baking powder, and pepper. Work quickly as the potato will begin to oxidize and brown.

Preheat the oven to warm. Heat a large non-stick skillet over medium-high and add the oil. For each latke, spoon ¼ cup (60 mL) potato mixture into oil, pressing down lightly with fork to flatten and leaving about 1 inch (2.5 cm) between latkes.

Fry the latkes until golden brown, crispy on the outside, and cooked through, 5–6 minutes per side. If the potato starts to scorch (burn), turn down the heat to medium or medium-low. Transfer cooked latkes to a baking sheet lined with paper towels and place in the oven. Repeat with the remaining batter. Serve warm.

3 cups (750 mL) white whole wheat flour (or all-purpose flour)
1 tsp (5 mL) sea salt
⅓ cup (75 mL) extra-virgin olive oil
1 cup (250 mL) warm water
½ cup (125 mL) wild seeds (onion, dock, mustard, etc.)

MAKES 2–3 DOZEN CRACKERS

WILD SEED CRACKERS

Wild seeds are packed with nutrition and flavour. I particularly like to save onion, dock, and mustard seeds along with abundant poppy seeds from the garden to make these thin and delicious crackers. Sesame seeds are also a nice addition to the mix.

In food processor, combine the flour and salt. Pulse the machine, then leave on and pour in the olive oil. Add the water in a steady stream until the dough comes together in a ball. Place on a floured work surface and add the seeds. Knead until the seeds are incorporated and the dough is smooth and elastic.

Divide dough into quarters, cover with olive oil, and place on a plate. Cover dough with plastic wrap and a kitchen towel. Allow to rest for 1 hour.

Preheat the oven to 400°F (200°C).

Place the dough on a floured surface and roll out with a rolling pin. Cut into squares or triangles, or leave in big pieces to break up later. Set on a baking sheet lined with parchment paper (or a silicone mat). You can top with a little beaten egg white and sprinkle with sea salt, additional wild seeds, sesame seeds, etc. Pierce all over with a fork to prevent puffing.

Place in the oven and bake for 5–7 minutes, or until golden brown. Keep an eye on the crackers as they bake, as each oven is a little different! Place them on a rack and allow to cool to room temperature. Store the crackers in an airtight container until needed.

2 cups (500 mL) all-purpose flour
1 tsp (5 mL) salt
2 eggs
2 cups (500 mL) cold water, divided
½ cup (125 mL) chopped wild onions (or green onions)
about ¼ cup (60 mL) vegetable oil, for frying

MAKES ABOUT 16 PANCAKES

NORTHERN CHINESE–STYLE WILD ONION PANCAKES

These thin pancakes are the Chinese version of a crepe. They are excellent with BBQ duck or pork, hoisin sauce, and shredded lettuce. Serve these fillings on platters and let guests roll their own pancakes. For a vegetarian version, substitute roasted squash or spicy fried tofu for the meats. In China, these crepes are traditionally served as street food and filled with pork, egg, and fried Chinese donut.

In a mixing bowl, combine the flour and salt. Make a well in the middle and add the eggs and 1 cup (250 mL) of the water. Whisk together until a smooth paste is formed. Add the remaining water and gently whisk until a smooth batter is formed. Fold in the wild onions. The batter should be thin enough to pour off a spoon. Thin down with additional water if it is too thick.

Preheat the oven to warm.

Heat a 10-inch skillet over medium for 1 minute. Add 1 teaspoon (5 mL) of the oil and swirl around the pan. Pour about ¼ cup (60 mL) of the batter into the skillet, swirling the skillet to evenly coat the bottom. Cook the pancake for about 1 minute, or until the batter firms and the bottom just begins to brown. Flip the pancake with a spatula and cook an additional minute on the second side. Transfer to a plate covered with a clean kitchen towel and place in the oven. Repeat with the remaining batter to make more pancakes, adding oil to the pan as needed.

BREAKFAST

4 large eggs
2 Tbsp (30 mL) water
salt and pepper, to taste
1 Tbsp (15 mL) butter (or olive oil)
1 small onion, peeled and diced
1 cup (250 mL) sliced fresh chanterelles
1 ear of corn, cooked and chilled
2 Tbsp (30 mL) chopped fresh cilantro (or parsley)
¼ cup (60 mL) shredded aged white cheddar

SERVES 2–4

CHANTERELLE, CORN, AND AGED CHEDDAR OMELETTE

This is an omelette to celebrate the clash of two seasons—the end of the local sweet corn crops and the first of the late-summer chanterelles. This dish is a tribute to the sweetness of the corn and the earthy forest flavours of the mushrooms. Use the best white cheddar you can find.

In a small bowl, combine the eggs and water. Whisk until combined and season with salt and pepper.

Heat a non-stick pan over medium-high and add the butter. Toss in the onion and chanterelles. Slice the corn kernels off the cob and add to the pan along with the cilantro, stirring to warm through. Add the eggs and swirl around the pan to coat the entire bottom. Reduce the heat to low, and when the eggs begin to set, take a spatula and gently push the eggs away from the side of the pan. Tilt the pan to allow any uncooked egg in the centre to flow to the edges. Swirl the pan to allow the egg to cover the bottom of the pan.

Add the cheese to one side of the omelette. Flip the opposite edge of the omelette over to cover the cheese. Cook for an additional 2 minutes to set the egg and warm the cheese. Slide onto a plate and flip so the side last in contact with the pan is on top (gives you a nicer presentation). Serve warm.

1 oz (28 g) dried morel mushrooms
½ lb (225 g) asparagus, trimmed
4 large eggs
2 Tbsp (30 mL) water
salt and pepper, to taste

1 Tbsp (15 mL) butter (or olive oil)
4 green onions, trimmed and
  chopped
¼ cup (60 mL) fresh goat cheese

SERVES 2–4

ASPARAGUS, GOAT CHEESE, AND MOREL OMELETTE

In many good professional kitchens, an omelette is the first test for the new cooks. It shows your level of technique, patience, and finesse when handling delicate ingredients. The first trick here is to lighten the egg with a little water when mixing. This allows the egg to fluff up and become tender. The second trick is to push back the egg from the sides and swirl the pan to remove the uncooked egg from the centre. With these tips, you'll be cooking like a pro in no time.

In a heatproof bowl (or glass measuring cup) add the morels and cover with hot tap water. Rinse immediately and cover a second time with hot water. Set aside to rehydrate for at least 15 minutes.

Meanwhile, bring a saucepan of water to a boil over high heat. Chop the asparagus into 1-inch (2.5 cm) pieces and add to the water along with a dash of salt. Boil for 5 minutes or until the asparagus is just tender. Strain and rinse with cold water. Set aside until needed.

In a small bowl, combine the eggs and water. Whisk until combined and season with salt and pepper.

Heat a non-stick pan over medium-high and add the butter. Toss in the green onions and asparagus. Drain the morels and chop coarsely into bite-size pieces. Add to the asparagus and toss to warm through. Add the eggs and swirl around the pan to coat the entire bottom. Reduce the heat to low and when the eggs begin to set, take a spatula and gently push the eggs away from the side of the pan. Tilt the pan to allow any uncooked egg in the centre to flow to the edges. Swirl the pan to allow the egg to cover the bottom of the pan.

Add the cheese to one side of the omelette. Flip the opposite edge of the omelette over to cover the cheese. Cook for an additional 2 minutes to set the egg and warm the cheese. Slide onto a plate and flip so the side last in contact with the pan is on top (gives you a nicer presentation). Serve warm.

4 large eggs

2 Tbsp (30 mL) water

salt and pepper, to taste

2 slices bacon, cut into thin strips

1 small onion, peeled and diced

1 large potato, peeled and shredded

2 cups (500 mL) oxeye daisy tops, coarsely chopped

1 tomato, cored and chopped

¼ cup (60 mL) shredded mozzarella cheese

SERVES 2–4

FRITTATA WITH POTATO, BACON, AND OXEYE DAISY GREENS

Leave it to the Italians to take all of the stress out of flipping an omelette. The secret here is to cook the egg partially (a little runny in the centre is fine). Top with the cheese and place under a broiler to melt the cheese and finish cooking the egg. This is a great dish for feeding a crowd for lunch or dinner. The dish is great with most types of greens. Blanched stinging nettle, lamb's quarters, and miner's lettuce are some of my favourites.

Preheat the broiler to high.

In a small bowl, combine the eggs and water. Whisk until combined and season with salt and pepper.

Heat a non-stick pan over medium-high and add the bacon, onion, and potato. Stir-fry for 5 minutes or until the bacon renders fat and the potato softens and begins to brown. Add the oxeye daisy tops, stirring to warm through. Add the eggs and swirl around the pan to coat the entire bottom. Reduce the heat to low and when the eggs begin to set, take a spatula and gently push the eggs away from the side of the pan. Tilt the pan to allow any uncooked egg in the centre to flow to the edges. Swirl the pan to allow the egg to cover the bottom of the pan.

Distribute the tomato over the egg and sprinkle on the grated cheese. Place the skillet under the broiler for 2–3 minutes or until the cheese is melted and beginning to brown in spots. Remove from the oven and allow to sit for 1–2 minutes. Portion and serve warm.

Sauce

2 cups (500 mL) stinging nettle tops
1 Tbsp (15 mL) butter
1 Tbsp (15 mL) all-purpose flour
1 cup (250 mL) milk
salt and pepper, to taste
¼ cup (60 mL) sour cream

1 Tbsp (15 mL) chopped fresh garlic
1 tsp (5 mL) vinegar
4 large eggs
2 English muffins
4 slices cooked ham (or turkey)
   (optional)

SERVES 4

POACHED EGGS WITH ENGLISH MUFFINS AND STINGING NETTLE SAUCE

Plucked from the pages of a Dr. Seuss book, these emerald green eggs are delicious and attractive on the table for breakfast, lunch, or dinner. For a deluxe version, I use sautéed mushrooms, smoked salmon, or Dungeness crab meat in place of the meat.

Soak the stinging nettles in plenty of cold water. Rinse and drain. Bring a large pot of salted water to a boil over high heat. Add the nettles and cook for 30 seconds or until the nettles are limp and dark green. Remove with a slotted spoon or tongs and transfer to a large bowl of cold water. Shock (chill) the nettles to stop the cooking process. Drain the nettles and squeeze out all moisture. You will end up with a small ball of nettles. Coarsely chop the nettles.

Heat a saucepan over medium-high and add the butter. When it sizzles, add the flour and whisk until smooth. Cook for 1 minute or until the mixture is bubbling. Add the milk and whisk until smooth. Reduce the heat to low and simmer for 5 minutes, or until the mixture thickens, stirring occasionally. Add the nettles and season with salt and pepper. Add the sour cream and garlic, stirring until distributed and smooth. You may serve as is, or you can purée with a hand blender for an even green colour. Keep warm and stir again just before use.

Heat a clean saucepan filled halfway with water over medium-high. Bring to a boil, reduce the heat to a simmer, and add the vinegar. Crack one of the eggs into a small container and add the egg to the water. Swirling the water with a spoon helps to keep the egg in a more compact shape. Repeat with remaining eggs. Poach for 4 minutes, or until the whites thicken and the yolk is still slightly runny.

Meanwhile, split the English muffin in half and toast. Lightly butter and place on a serving plate. Top each half with a little cooked ham (if using). Remove an egg from the water with a slotted spoon. Pat the spoon on a paper or cloth towel to wick excess moisture off the egg. Place the egg on top of the ham. Spoon a little sauce overtop of the egg. Repeat with the remaining eggs and muffins. Serve warm. Any extra sauce is good with cooked vegetables, such as asparagus, leeks, or cauliflower.

8 cups (2 L) stinging nettle tops (or spinach)
1 Tbsp (15 mL) butter (or olive oil)
2 onions, peeled and thinly sliced
2 stalks celery, diced
1 Tbsp (15 mL) minced garlic
4 green onions, trimmed and thinly sliced
2 Tbsp (30 mL) mixed herbs (thyme, sage, parsley)
salt and pepper, to taste
6 large eggs
4 cups (1 L) milk (or cream)
6 cups (1.5 mL) thinly sliced French bread or baguette
1 cup (250 mL) diced smoked salmon
2 cups (500 mL) grated mozzarella or Swiss cheese

MAKES 8 PORTIONS

SMOKED SALMON AND STINGING NETTLE STRATA

A strata is a kind of savoury bread pudding. The best bread for this dish is white flour bread, which gives you a soft and soufflé-like texture. I often use large loafs of French bread (called bâtards). This is a good use for stale bread or extra loves you have stashed in the freezer. You can use almost any type of bread with good results. I also use smoked salmon chunks, sometimes sold as ends, which are cheaper alternatives that you can find in some of the markets. If you can't find them, you can substitute candied salmon or make your own from pink or chum salmon.

Soak the stinging nettles in plenty of cold water. Rinse and drain. Bring a large pot of salted water to boil over high heat. Add the nettles and cook for 30 seconds, or until the nettles are limp and dark green. Remove with a slotted spoon or tongs and transfer to a large bowl of cold water. Shock (chill) the nettles to stop the cooking process. Drain the nettles and squeeze out all moisture. You will end up with a softball-sized lump of nettle.

Preheat oven to 325°F (160°C).

Heat a sauté pan over medium-high and add the butter, onions, and celery. Sauté until the onions soften and begin to give off moisture. Add the garlic, green onions, and herbs, and season with salt and pepper. Set aside to cool.

STINGING NETTLE

In a mixing bowl, add the eggs and whisk to mix. Add the milk and whisk well to blend. Season well with salt and pepper.

Place a layer of bread in a large casserole dish. Sprinkle with a little of the smoked salmon and a sprinkling of the onion mixture. Chop the cooked stinging nettles into a course dice. Sprinkle a little of the nettles over the bread. Repeat with remaining salmon and vegetables. Pour the egg mixture over the bread, pushing down with a spoon to ensure all the slices are soaked with the mixture. Sprinkle the grated cheese evenly overtop. Place in the oven for 45 minutes, or until set and slightly browned on top. Remove from the oven and allow to sit for at least 10 minutes. Cut into squares (or scoop with a large spoon) and serve warm.

2 cups (500 mL) sliced fresh mushrooms (chanterelle, porcini, etc.)

2 Tbsp (30 mL) butter, divided

1 Tbsp (15 mL) chopped fresh rosemary

salt and pepper, to taste

4 slices French bread cut from a loaf (2 inches [5 cm] thick)

4 slices ham (or turkey)

4 slices Swiss or Gruyère cheese

2 eggs

1 cup (250 mL) milk

SERVES 4

MUSHROOM-STUFFED FRENCH TOAST

This dish is probably closer to a Monte Cristo sandwich than a traditional plate of French toast, but it is a wonderful flavour combination for a savoury breakfast. You can make a batch for a crowd and keep the toast warm in advance of your guests arriving. Cut into small wedges, this dish makes a great appetizer for gathering or parties.

Heat a non-stick pan over medium-high and add the mushrooms and 1 tablespoon (15 mL) of the butter. Season well with rosemary, salt, and pepper. Toss to coat and sauté until the mushrooms give off moisture and cook until the pan appears dry again. Remove from the heat and allow to cool to room temperature.

Place the slices of bread on a cutting board. With a bread knife, make a cut through one side of each slice, three quarters of the way through. Into each of these pockets, stuff a quarter of the ham, cheese, and mushrooms.

In a mixing bowl, combine the eggs and milk. Season with salt and pepper and whisk to mix well. Dip the stuffed bread into the batter and briefly let it soak. Heat a non-stick skillet over medium-high and add the remaining butter. Swirl to coat the pan and add the dipped slices of bread. Cook until golden brown, about 5 minutes per side, reducing the heat if they brown too quickly. Transfer to a plate and let rest in a warm oven until ready to serve warm.

1½ cups (375 mL) all-purpose flour
3 Tbsp (45 mL) sugar
1 tsp (5 mL) baking powder
1 tsp (5 mL) baking soda
¼ tsp (1 mL) salt
1¾ cups (425 mL) buttermilk
1 egg
2 Tbsp (30 mL) melted butter
2 tsp (10 mL) vanilla
1 Tbsp (15 mL) vegetable oil
2 cups (500 mL) wild berries (blueberries, blackberries, etc.)

SERVES 4

WILD BERRY PANCAKES

This is another classic use for wild fruit that is very easy to make. Once you try the results, you will throw away any commercial pancake mixes in your cupboard. If you want to pump up the wild component, you can add cattail pollen, cooked wild rice, or chopped hazelnuts to the batter. I sometimes add wild herbs to the batter and make savoury pancakes that are great topped with smoked salmon and sour cream.

Preheat the oven to warm.

In a large bowl, whisk together the flour, sugar, baking powder, baking soda, and salt. In another bowl, whisk together the buttermilk, egg, melted butter, and vanilla; pour over the dry ingredients. Whisk until combined but still slightly lumpy.

Heat a large non-stick skillet or griddle over medium-high; lightly brush with some of the oil. Pour batter, ¼ cup (60 mL) at a time, into the pan; spread slightly to form pancakes. Sprinkle each pancake with berries to cover the top.

Cook until bubbles appear on top, about 3 minutes. Flip and cook until the bottoms are golden brown, about 1 minute. Transfer to a serving plate, cover, and keep warm in the oven until all the pancakes are cooked.

4 eggs, room temperature

1 cup (250 mL) milk, at room temperature

1 cup (250 mL) all-purpose flour

1 tsp (5 mL) pure vanilla extract

3 Tbsp (45 mL) grapeseed oil

2 Tbsp (30 mL) butter, divided

2 cups (500 mL) wild berries (blackberries, blueberries, etc.)

2 Tbsp (30 mL) maple syrup

MAKES 4 SERVINGS

SOUFFLÉ PANCAKES WITH WARM MAPLE BERRIES

This classic breakfast dish is basically a sweet version of a Yorkshire pudding. You sometimes hear it referred to as a "Dutch baby." The pancake is great with just maple syrup and butter, but it is also delicious with any of the wild syrups or jams from the pantry section.

Preheat the oven to 400°F (200°C).

In a mixing bowl, combine the eggs and milk; whisk to mix evenly. Add the flour and stir until the mixture just comes together smoothly. Add the vanilla extract and set aside.

Heat a large cast-iron skillet over medium-high and add the oil and 1 tablespoon (15 mL) of the butter. When the butter is sizzling and the oil is hot, pour in the batter. Transfer the skillet to the hot oven and bake for 20 minutes or until the pancake has puffed up considerably and is golden brown.

Meanwhile, heat a saucepan over medium and add the remaining butter. Add the berries and maple syrup. Reduce the heat to a simmer and keep warm while the pancake is cooking. When the pancake is ready, remove the skillet from the oven and transfer to the table. Scoop out servings of pancake with a spoon and serve immediately with the warm berry sauce.

SALADS

8 cups (2 L) stinging nettle tops
2 Tbsp (30 mL) soy sauce
1 Tbsp (15 mL) grapeseed oil
1 tsp (5 mL) sesame oil
1 Tbsp (15 mL) mirin
1 Tbsp (15 mL) white sesame seeds

SERVES 4–6

STINGING NETTLE GOMAE

Gomae translates to "sesame" in Japanese and is usually a dish made with spinach. I have also had great results with lamb's quarters, miner's lettuce, chickweed, and burdock leaves. In particular, the slightly bitter greens benefit from the infusion of sesame, soy, and sweet mirin (made from sweetened sake).

Soak the stinging nettles in plenty of cold water. Rinse and drain. Bring a large pot of salted water to boil over high heat. Add the nettles and cook for 30 seconds, or until the nettles are limp and dark green. Remove with a slotted spoon or tongs and transfer to a large bowl of cold water. Shock (chill) the nettles to stop the cooking process. Drain the nettles and squeeze out all moisture. You will end up with a softball-sized lump of nettles. Coarsely chop the nettles.

In a mixing bowl, add the soy sauce, grapeseed oil, sesame oil, and mirin. Whisk until uniform, then add the nettles and sesame seeds and toss well to mix. Let sit for 5 minutes and serve at room temperature. This mixture will keep for several days in the refrigerator.

1 package (about ½ lb [225 g]) soba noodles (or see p. 167)
1 Tbsp (15 mL) grapeseed oil
1 Tbsp (15 mL) minced fresh garlic
2 cups (250 mL) sliced mushrooms (pine, cauliflower fungus, oysters, etc.)
2 Tbsp (30 mL) soy sauce (infused with bonito and seaweed if possible)
juice and zest of 1 lemon
1 Tbsp (15 mL) mirin
1 Tbsp (15 mL) brown sugar
2 cups (500 mL) shredded lettuce
shredded nori, for garnish
sesame seeds, for garnish

SERVES 4

MUSHROOM AND SOBA NOODLE SALAD

Soba noodles are made from grains of buckwheat (a type of grass) and are a revered cultural dish in Japan where they are often eaten chilled with a vinegar and soy dipping sauce flavoured with bonito (smoked fish) and kombu seaweed. You can sometimes find soy sauce infused with these ingredients in Japanese markets.

In a large pot of boiling salted water, cook the soba until just tender (al dente). Drain and spread onto a tray to cool (you can lightly coat with oil to help keep the strands separated).

In a sauté pan over medium-high heat, add the grapeseed oil and garlic. When sizzling, add the mushrooms and sauté for 3–4 minutes, or until they release their moisture and the pan has evaporated most of the juice.

In a mixing bowl, combine the soy sauce, lemon juice, lemon zest, mirin, and brown sugar. Stir well to mix. Add the noodles, mushrooms, and lettuce; toss well to coat. Transfer to a serving plate (or bowl) and garnish with the nori and sesame seeds and serve immediately. This is a dish traditionally eaten with chopsticks. It should also be eaten quickly to preserve the texture of the soba (which will become soft and soggy as it sits in the sauce).

Chickpeas

1 Tbsp (15 mL) extra-virgin olive oil

4 cups (1 L) cooked chickpeas

1 Tbsp (15 mL) chopped fresh garlic

1 tsp (5 mL) hot sauce

juice and zest of 1 lemon

Dressing

1 Tbsp (15 mL) rosehip butter (p. 80)

1 Tbsp (15 mL) prepared mustard

1 Tbsp (15 mL) white wine vinegar

¼ cup (60 mL) yogurt

4 cups (1 L) wild greens (or mixed salad greens)

salt and pepper, to taste

toasted sunflower seeds, for garnish

SERVES 4–6

SPICY GARLIC CHICKPEAS WITH WILD GREENS AND ROSEHIP YOGURT DRESSING

This salad is best with milder greens like miner's lettuce, oxeye daisy tops, and peppercress leaves. For extra crispy chickpeas, toss them in a little potato starch before sautéing.

In a skillet over medium-high heat, add the olive oil and chickpeas. Sauté until the chickpeas begin to brown and crisp up. Add the garlic and hot sauce and sauté until the garlic just begins to brown. Add the lemon juice and zest to the pan and sauté until the pan appears dry. Remove from the heat and set aside to cool.

In a salad bowl, combine the rosehip purée, mustard, vinegar, and yogurt. Whisk to mix. Add the greens and the cooled chickpeas to the bowl. Season with salt and pepper; toss well to coat. Garnish with toasted sunflower seeds and serve chilled or at room temperature.

1 Tbsp (15 mL) grapeseed oil
2 cups (500 mL) sliced chanterelle mushrooms
1 Tbsp (15 mL) minced fresh garlic
1 red onion, peeled and diced
salt and pepper, to taste
4 ears of corn, cooked and chilled
2 cups (500 mL) cooked black beans
2 cups (500 mL) shredded green cabbage
1 large carrot, peeled and shredded
juice and zest of 1 lime
2 Tbsp (30 mL) extra-virgin olive oil
1 tsp (5 mL) hot sauce
3 Tbsp (45 mL) minced cilantro

SERVES 4–6

CHANTERELLE, BLACK BEAN, AND CORN SALAD

This is a perfect dish for picnics or backyard dining. It works well with chanterelles or any type of mushroom you have on hand. If you like more spice, add more hot sauce or minced hot peppers to the salad. Cooking the red onion slightly removes a little of the bitter edge and enhances the sweetness.

Heat a skillet over medium-high and add the grapeseed oil, mushrooms, and garlic. Sauté until the mushrooms give off moisture and appear dry. Add the red onion and toss to warm through but not cook fully, about 1–2 minutes. Transfer to a mixing bowl, season with salt and pepper and allow to cool to room temperature.

On a cutting board, trim the kernels off the ears of corn. Add to the mushrooms along with the black beans, cabbage, and carrot. Add the lime zest and juice to the vegetables. Drizzle with olive oil and hot sauce. Add the cilantro and toss to coat. Taste and adjust the seasoning with salt and pepper if necessary. Serve chilled or at room temperature.

1 cup (250 mL) red quinoa

3 Tbsp (45 mL) extra-virgin olive oil, divided

2 cups (500 mL) vegetable broth

1 small seedless cucumber, diced

1 red pepper, seeded and diced

½ cup (125 mL) chopped pickled cattail shoots (p. 88)

1 cup (250 mL) Thompson raisins, soaked in water

1 Tbsp (15 mL) white wine vinegar

2 Tbsp (30 mL) chopped fresh parsley (or chives)

salt and pepper, to taste

SERVES 4

QUINOA SALAD WITH PICKLED CATTAIL AND RAISINS

Quinoa was a traditional wild food harvested in the mountains of South America. It is the seed of a plant that is closely related to beets and spinach. The red variety has a slight nutty flavour. Cattail is best when picked in the early summer, when new shoots of the plant sprout up 2–3 feet in height.

Place quinoa in a saucepan and rinse well under cold water; let sit for 5 minutes. Drain into a fine mesh sieve and allow to sit until well drained. Heat the saucepan over medium-high and add 1 tablespoon (15 mL) of the olive oil. Add the quinoa and gently toast until the grains begin to stick to the bottom. Add the vegetable broth and bring to a boil. Lower the heat to a bare simmer and cover with a tight-fitting lid. Cook for 10 minutes, then remove from the heat and allow to sit for an additional 5 minutes.

In a salad bowl, combine the cucumber, red pepper, and cattail. Drain the raisins and add to the bowl. Top with the cooked quinoa and stir to mix. Add the remaining 2 tablespoons (30 mL) of olive oil, the vinegar, and the parsley. Season with salt and pepper and serve chilled or at room temperature.

1 lb (454 g) new nugget potatoes
1 lb (454 g) asparagus
salt and pepper, to taste
juice and zest of 1 lemon
1 tsp (5 mL) honey
2 Tbsp (30 mL) extra-virgin olive oil
¼ cup (60 mL) chopped wild mint leaves

SERVES 4

WILD MINT, ASPARAGUS, AND NEW POTATO SALAD

This salad is perfect for early summer, when the wild mint is blooming, the asparagus is plump, and the first new potatoes hit the market. The dish is a wonderful combination of fresh flavours and highlights the sweetness of these beautiful seasonal products.

Bring a large pot of salted water to a boil. Add the potatoes and cook for 5 minutes. Meanwhile, take the asparagus spears and snap off the tough ends. Chop the remaining asparagus into 2-inch (5 cm) pieces. Add the asparagus to the potatoes and continue cooking until the potatoes are tender and the asparagus is just cooked, about 5–7 minutes.

Drain the vegetables into a colander and run under cold water briefly. Set aside to drain. When cool enough to handle, coarsely slice the potato into rounds and add to a mixing bowl. Add the cooked asparagus and season with salt and pepper. In a small bowl, combine the lemon juice, lemon zest, and honey. Stir to dissolve the honey and whisk in the olive oil. Pour over the potatoes, add the chopped mint, and toss to coat. Check the seasoning and add more salt and pepper if necessary. Serve chilled or at room temperature.

SIDE DISHES

2 lb (about 1 kg) russet potatoes, scrubbed
1 tsp (5 mL) salt
4 Tbsp (60 mL) butter
¼ cup (60 mL) whipping cream (or milk), warmed
2 Tbsp (30 mL) finely minced wild onions
salt and pepper, to taste
1 Tbsp (15 mL) minced fresh parsley

SERVES 4

MASHED POTATOES WITH WILD ONIONS

Use baker or russet potatoes for the lightest and fluffiest mashed potatoes. Use a potato ricer (a potato press) to squeeze the potato into a paste. A food mill also works well. Using a mixer overworks the potato, causing the starches to become sticky and giving it a gummy texture. Lightly working the potato will give you an incredibly silky mash.

Rinse the potatoes and place them in a large saucepan. Cover them with cold water and lightly salt the water. Bring to a boil, reduce the heat to medium, and cook for 20 minutes, or until a potato is easily pierced with a fork.

Drain the water, cool until you can just handle the potatoes, and peel them. While still warm, mash potatoes with a ricer, food mill, or masher. Return to a saucepan and add butter, cream, and onion. Stir well to mix until smooth and creamy. Season well with salt and pepper and fold in the parsley. Can be made in advance and kept warm until needed (cover and hold for up to 1 hour in a warm oven). If the potato firms up, thin with a little more warm cream or milk until a soft mash is obtained. Serve warm.

1 lb (454 g) dried small white beans
1 ham hock (about 1 lb [454 g])
1 cup (250 mL) tomato paste
¼ cup (60 mL) bigleaf maple syrup
2 Tbsp (30 mL) molasses
2 Tbsp (30 mL) garlic
1 cup (250 mL) peeled and diced
  carrots

1 cup (250 mL) peeled and diced
  onion
1 cup (250 mL) diced celery
¼ cup (60 mL) apple cider vinegar
1 Tbsp (15 mL) finely minced fresh
  rosemary
1 Tbsp (15 mL) hot sauce
salt and pepper, to taste

SERVES 4–6

BAKED MAPLE BEAN CASSEROLE

I love to use a small French bean called the flageolet, a small bean with a light, green-white hue and a wonderful firm and creamy flesh. If you are unable to source these beans you can use a commonly available variety like great northern or white navy beans. I use bigleaf maple syrup or substitute dark maple syrup.

Soak the beans in water for at least 1 hour (overnight is best). Discard the water, transfer the beans to a pot, and cover with cold water. Bring to a boil over medium-high heat. Reduce the heat and simmer for 30 minutes. Add the ham hock and simmer for an additional 30 minutes, or until the beans are tender. Remove from the heat and allow to cool completely.

Preheat the oven to 350°F (180°C).

Remove the ham hock from the water. Trim off any skin and fat, and remove the bones; discard. Cut the meat into a fine mince; set aside until needed.

Strain the beans and reserve 2 cups (500 mL) of the cooking liquid. Transfer the beans to a casserole dish and set aside. In a saucepan, combine the tomato paste, maple syrup, molasses, garlic, carrots, onion, celery, vinegar, rosemary, hot sauce, minced ham, and reserved bean-cooking liquid. Bring to a boil, then reduce the heat to a simmer and cook for 15 minutes. Pour the sauce over the bean mixture and stir well. Season well with salt and pepper. Place in the oven and bake for 1 hour, stirring occasionally. Serve warm.

2 cups (500 mL) short-grained
  sticky rice
4 cups (1 L) water
2 slices fresh ginger
2 lb (about 1 kg) mussels
¼ cup (60 mL) white wine
1 Tbsp (15 mL) grapeseed oil
1 medium onion, peeled and diced
2 cups (500 mL) chopped broccoli

1 red pepper, cored, seeded, and
  diced
1 Tbsp (15 mL) curry paste
1 Tbsp (15 mL) minced fresh
  ginger
1 Tbsp (15 mL) minced fresh garlic
1 can (14 oz [400 mL]) coconut milk
¼ cup (60 mL) chopped cilantro,
  basil, or mint, for garnish

SERVE 4–6

STICKY RICE CASSEROLE WITH MUSSELS AND COCONUT CURRY

This dish takes a bit of preparation but the results are outstanding, even improving over the next couple of days (assuming there are leftovers!). Mussels are best cooked live, with their shells tightly closed. Discard any opened mussels before cooking (pinch them closed and discard those that quickly pop back open).

In a medium pot (one with a tight-fitting lid), rinse the rice under cold water, rubbing it with your hands to release the starch. Rinse until the water becomes relatively clear. Drain, then add the measured water and ginger slices. Place the pot over high heat and bring the water to a boil. Reduce the heat to low, cover the pot, and cook for 20 minutes. Remove the pot from the heat and let stand for 10 minutes.

Heat a large saucepan over medium-high and add the mussels and wine. As the mussels open, remove from the pot and transfer to a bowl. Repeat with remaining mussels. If after 5 minutes of cooking any mussels have not opened, you may discard them. Reserve the cooking liquid. Remove the mussels from their shells and the reserve meat.

Preheat the oven to 350°F (180°C).

Heat a large skillet over medium-high and add the grapeseed oil, onion, broccoli, and red pepper. Sauté until the onion begins to brown. Add the curry paste, minced ginger, and garlic and sauté for an additional 1–2 minutes. Add the coconut milk and reserved mussel juice (discard any sediment that settles to the bottom of the mussel juice). Reduce the heat to a simmer and cook for 5 minutes, or until the vegetables are tender.

Place the rice in a large casserole dish. Add the reserved mussels and toss to coat. Pour the curry sauce overtop of the rice and mussels. Bake in the oven for 30 minutes, or until bubbling and beginning to brown on top. Serve warm, garnished with fresh cilantro, basil, or mint.

Sauce

3 Tbsp (45 mL) mayonnaise

1 tsp (5 mL) hot sauce

1 tsp (5 mL) sesame oil

1 tsp (5 mL) wasabi paste

2 Tbsp (30 mL) minced green onion

1 Tbsp (15 mL) grapeseed oil

4 cups (1 L) chopped wild greens (lamb's quarters, miner's lettuce, etc.)

1 tsp (5 mL) sesame oil

salt and pepper, to taste

1 recipe wild sushi rice (p. 150)

1 lb (454 g) spot prawn tails, shell on

1 Tbsp (15 mL) toasted sesame seeds, for garnish

SERVES 4–6

WARM WILD SUSHI AND FORAGED GREENS WITH SPOT PRAWNS

Traditional country-style sushi was used as a preservation technique to allow workers to bring a rice lunch into the hot fields. This rustic presentation provides amazing sushi flavours without the skill needed to roll or mould those perfect classical forms. This dish is also great with wild greens like blanched stinging nettles or spicier greens like wild mustard.

In a small bowl, combine the mayonnaise, hot sauce, sesame oil, wasabi paste, and green onion. Stir well and season with salt and pepper (if needed).

Heat a large, non-stick pan over high and add the grapeseed oil and greens. Toss until wilted, about 1 minute. Season with sesame oil, salt, and pepper. Place in a mixing bowl, add the sushi rice, and toss well to mix.

Place the prawns in a heatproof bowl and cover with boiling water. Let sit for 5 minutes and drain. Remove the shells and set the prawns aside until needed.

Transfer the rice mixture to serving bowls; top with the cooked prawns. Garnish with a dollop of sauce and sesame seeds. Serve immediately.

3 large eggs
1 tsp (5 mL) sesame oil
1 tsp (5 mL) soy sauce
2 Tbsp (30 mL) grapeseed oil, divided
4 cups (1 L) chopped wild greens (miner's lettuce, purslane, oxeye daisy, etc.)
4 green onions, thinly sliced
1 Tbsp (15 mL) minced garlic
4 cups (1 L) cooked rice (short-grain brown or your favourite rice)
2 Tbsp (30 mL) sesame seeds
additional soy sauce, at the table

SERVES 4–6

FRIED RICE WITH WILD GREENS AND EGG

This dish is a favourite use of pre-cooked or leftover rice. I particularly like to use short-grain brown rice for its chewy texture and healthy fibre. Use almost any wild green in this dish: even more bitter varieties like dandelion are excellent when stir-fried with rice.

In a small mixing bowl, combine the eggs, sesame oil, and soy sauce. Whisk to blend.

Heat a non-stick skillet over medium-high and add 1 tablespoon (15 mL) of the grapeseed oil. Add the eggs and swirl to coat the bottom of the pan. Cook for 2 minutes or until the egg firms up. Flip the egg and cook the second side for an additional minute. Transfer to a plate and allow to cool.

Return the skillet to the heat and add the remaining grapeseed oil. Add the greens, green onion, and garlic. Sauté until the greens wilt, about 1 minute. Add the rice and toss to distribute the greens. Cook until the rice begins to soften and brown slightly on the bottom. Add the sesame seeds and season with salt and pepper.

Chop the egg into bite-size chunks and add to the rice. Stir the rice to distribute the egg. Transfer to a serving plate and serve with additional soy sauce.

1 cup (250 mL) sushi rice
2 cups (500 mL) water
2 Tbsp (30 mL) rice vinegar
1 tsp (5 mL) sugar
1 tsp (5 mL) salt
1 cup (250 mL) cooked wild rice (see Chef's Tip)

MAKES ABOUT 3 CUPS (750 ML)

WILD SUSHI RICE

Sushi rice is traditionally made with short-grain rice with a healthy dose of rice starch. Wild rice adds a crunchy texture and a nice, nutty flavour to the rice. It also makes for a dramatic presentation on the plate.

In a medium pot (one with a tight-fitting lid), rinse the sushi rice under cold water, rubbing with your hands to release the starch. Rinse until the water becomes relatively clear. Drain, then add the measured water. Place over high heat and bring to a boil. Reduce the heat to low, cover the pot, and cook the rice for 20 minutes. Remove the pot from the heat and let stand for 10 minutes.

Place the rice vinegar, sugar, and salt in a small bowl. Stir well to mix. Turn the sushi rice out onto a large baking sheet (or into a bowl), add the cooked wild rice, and sprinkle with the vinegar mixture. With a wooden utensil, stir the rice until it is well mixed and beginning to cool. Cover with a clean towel and keep at room temperature until needed.

Chef's Tip: To cook wild rice, it is best to soak the rice in cold water for several hours before cooking. Then strain and cover with cold water. Bring to a boil, reduce the heat, and simmer for 20 minutes. Turn off the heat and let sit for an additional 20 minutes. Strain the rice and continue with the recipe.

SOUPS & STOCKS

4 cups (1 L) water
1 (4-inch [10 cm]) square kombu (bull kelp)
1 oz (28 g) bonito flakes (or dried katsuobushi flakes)

MAKES 4 CUPS (1 L)

DASHI STOCK

Dashi is a quick, nutritious stock that is the foundation of many classics of Japanese cuisine. It is the foundation for miso soup, the base for steamed clams, and a great poaching liquid for vegetables and tofu. Authentic Japanese dashi is made with dried and smoked skipjack tuna (katsuobushi). Bonito is a cheaper substitute that is often more readily available in North America.

Place the water and kombu in a saucepan over medium heat. Bring slowly to a boil. Just before the water comes to a rolling boil, remove the kombu (otherwise a scum may form on the surface of the liquid). Add the bonito flakes and turn off the heat.

After the flakes have sunk to the bottom, strain the stock through a fine mesh sieve. A secondary broth may be made from the bonito, often used in stews.

Let cool. Place in covered container and keep for up to 4 days. May be frozen in cubes and used as needed for up to 2 months.

4 lb (about 2 kg) chicken back and neck bones
1 cup (250 mL) peeled and chopped onions
1 cup (250 mL) peeled and chopped carrots
1 cup (250 mL) chopped celery
1 handful fresh wild herbs (oxeye daisy, peppercress, etc.)
2 garlic cloves, chopped
1 tsp (5 mL) salt
4 quarts (4 L) cold water (enough to completely cover the bones)

MAKES 4 QUARTS (4 L)

CHICKEN STOCK WITH WILD HERBS

A good chicken stock has its place as the foundation for many great soups and sauces. The gelatin extracted from the bones is a key element. It coats your mouth and allows the other flavours to linger a little longer. The wild herbs add to the complexity of flavour and add excellent nutrients to the liquid. Make this stock in batches and keep in the freezer for up to 1 month.

Place the bones in a pot or large bowl and cover with water. Let soak for at least 10 minutes, then drain, rinse with fresh cold water, and drain again.

In a large stockpot, add the bones, onions, carrots, celery, wild herbs, garlic, and salt. Cover the bones with the measured cold water. Bring to a boil, then reduce to a simmer. Gently simmer the stock for 1–2 hours.

Pour the stock through a strainer into a storage container and let cool to room temperature. When cool, cover and place in the refrigerator to chill (overnight is best). The fat will congeal on the top and then can be easily removed. The stock should thicken from the gelatin in the skin and bones. Use in your favourite recipe or place in freezer bags and freeze for up to 3 months. There might be a layer of sediment that forms on the bottom of the chilled stock—this is protein and congealed blood and can be discarded.

16 cups (4 L) water
2 cups (500 mL) wild onions, trimmed
2 cups (500 mL) burdock root, trimmed and peeled
¼ cup (60 mL) dried porcini mushrooms
2 cups (500 mL) miner's lettuce
2 cups (500 mL) lamb's quarters
2 cups (500 mL) sheep sorrel
2 garlic cloves, peeled and chopped
1 tsp (5 mL) salt

MAKES 4 QUARTS (4 L)

FORAGED VEGETABLE BROTH

This is a great stock to make in the springtime and freeze in 1-quart (1 L) containers for later use in quick soups and sauces. If you want to add a little sweetness, add a couple of carrots or parsnips to the pot. Prepare the wild greens by trimming off any woody stems or diseased leaves and soaking the greens in a large container of water. This broth is filled with nutrients and potent immune system builders—treat it like nutritional gold.

Place a large stockpot over medium-high heat and add the water. Add the wild onions, burdock root, dried porcini, miner's lettuce, lamb's quarters, sheep sorrel, garlic, and salt. Bring to a boil, then reduce to a simmer. Gently simmer stock for 1 hour.

Pour through a strainer into a storage container and allow to cool to room temperature. When cool, cover and place in the refrigerator to chill (overnight is best). There might be a layer of sediment that forms on the bottom of the chilled stock; this can be discarded.

4 quarts (4 L) water
½ cup (125 mL) dried porcini mushrooms (or oyster, shiitake, etc.)
2 cups (500 mL) whole button mushrooms
1 cup (250 mL) peeled and chopped onions
1 cup (250 mL) peeled and chopped carrots
1 cup (250 mL) chopped celery
4 garlic cloves, roughly chopped
1 Tbsp (15 mL) chopped fresh rosemary
1 Tbsp (15 mL) chopped fresh sage

MAKES 4 QUARTS (4 L)

MUSHROOM VEGETABLE BROTH

This is a fast and delicious broth for adding flavour to sauces and soups. Shiitake mushrooms are always in my cupboard and are an excellent source of immune-system-boosting nutrients. This makes great use of a batch of oyster mushrooms. You can retrieve the mushrooms from the spent vegetables and chop them into the broth for more flavour and a great texture.

In a large stockpot, combine all the ingredients. Bring to a boil, reduce the heat, and simmer uncovered for 1 hour.

Strain the stock into a container and remove the mushrooms. Discard the rest of the vegetables and the herbs. The mushrooms may be sliced thinly and returned to the broth.

Place the container on a wire rack and let the stock cool to room temperature, then refrigerate in a covered container. Keeps for 3–4 days in the refrigerator, or for up to 3 months when frozen.

shells from 1–2 Dungeness crabs
1 cup (250 mL) chopped carrots
1 cup (250 mL) chopped celery
1 cup (250 mL) chopped onion
8 cups (2 L) water
4 slices fresh ginger
1 Tbsp (15 mL) miso paste

MAKES ABOUT 2 QUARTS (2 L)

CRAB STOCK

See the crab preparation technique on p. 68. One large crab will yield about 3 cups (750 mL) of crab shells. You can use an equal amount of spot prawn shells and heads to make another version of this excellent stock. This stock can form the base for a great crab bisque or can be used to cook rice (use in place of the water).

Preheat the oven to 350°F (180°C). Place the shells on a baking tray and place in the oven. Roast the shells for 10 minutes, or until they have lightly browned. Add the carrots, celery, and onion to the tray and roast for an additional 10 minutes.

Transfer the shells and vegetables to a stockpot and cover with the water. Add the ginger and miso paste. Bring to a boil, reduce the heat, and simmer for 1 hour. Strain the stock, allow to cool, and refrigerate or freeze until needed. Will keep for 3–4 days in the refrigerator, or up to 1 month in the freezer.

4 cups (1 L) stinging nettles

4 cups (1 L) dashi stock (p. 152) (or water)

2 Tbsp (30 mL) light miso

1 chunk (4 in [10 cm]) bull kelp

2 slices fresh ginger

1 Tbsp (15 mL) light soy sauce (or tamari)

½ lb (225 g) fresh soba noodles (p. 167) (or dried soba noodles)

SERVES 4

NETTLE MISO SOUP WITH SOBA NOODLES

In many Asian cultures, miso soup is used like our North American chicken noodle soup—a cure for most little ailments in life. If you have a few clams or mussels around, they are a wonderful addition to the broth.

Soak the stinging nettles in plenty of cold water. Rinse and drain. Bring a large pot of salted water to a boil over high heat. Add the nettles and cook for 30 seconds, or until the nettles are limp and dark green. Remove with a slotted spoon or tongs and transfer to a large bowl of cold water. Shock (chill) the nettles to stop the cooking process. Drain the nettles and squeeze out all moisture. You will end up with a small ball of nettles. Coarsely chop the nettles.

In a saucepan, add the dashi stock, miso, kelp, ginger, and soy sauce. Bring to a boil. Let sit for 10 minutes. Remove the kelp and ginger. Discard the ginger; shred the kelp and set aside. Bring the broth back to a boil. Add the cooked nettles and bring to a boil. Purée the soup with a hand blender until smooth. Add the kelp and bring back to a boil. Reduce the heat and simmer while you cook the noodles.

In a large pot, bring salted water to a boil. Add the soba noodles and immediately stir to separate the noodles. Bring to a boil, reduce the heat to stop foaming, and cook for 5–6 minutes, or until just tender. Drain the noodles and transfer to serving bowls. Top with the stinging nettle broth and serve with chopsticks and a spoon.

1 Tbsp (15 mL) extra-virgin olive oil
1 cup (250 mL) diced onions
1 cup (250 mL) diced celery
4 Tbsp (60 mL) minced garlic
2 cups (500 mL) diced oyster mushrooms (or chanterelle, button, etc.)
2 quarts (2 L) mushroom vegetable broth (p. 155) (or water)
1 cup (250 mL) diced dried bread (French bread is best)
2 Tbsp (30 mL) fresh chopped sage (or flat-leaf parsley)
additional extra-virgin olive oil, for garnish

SERVES 4–6

BREAD, OYSTER MUSHROOM, AND GARLIC SOUP

This soup is based on a traditional Portuguese bread and garlic soup. The addition of oyster mushrooms elevates this soup greatly. Feel free to add more garlic at the end of the cooking time for extra bite. For an extra touch of richness, you can add a softly poached egg to the final plating of the soup. This soup is also great the next day, although you may have to dilute it with more broth or water to get the right texture.

Heat a large soup pot over medium-high. Add the oil, onions, celery, and garlic. Sauté until the onions soften and just begin to brown. Add the mushrooms and continue to cook until all moisture is evaporated, about 5 minutes.

Add the broth and bring the soup to a boil. Add the bread and sage. Bring back to a simmer and cook until the bread breaks down and forms a thick soup, about 10 minutes. Ladle into bowls and drizzle with olive oil. Serve warm.

1 Tbsp (15 mL) grapeseed oil
1 cup (250 mL) diced onions
¼ cup (60 mL) dried porcini
   mushrooms
4 cups (1 L) diced fresh
   mushrooms (chanterelle,
   porcini, button, etc.)
1 cup (250 mL) diced potato
1 cup (250 mL) diced celery
2 Tbsp (30 mL) minced garlic
4 quarts (4 L) chicken stock
   (or water)

1 Tbsp (15 mL) minced fresh
   rosemary
1 Tbsp (15 mL) minced fresh sage
1 Tbsp (15 mL) minced fresh thyme
1 cup (250 mL) whipping cream
salt and pepper, to taste

Topping

1 cup (250 mL) sour cream
1 Tbsp (15 mL) porcini powder
   (p. 19)
1 Tbsp (15 mL) balsamic vinegar
minced chives, for garnish

SERVES 6–8

WILD MUSHROOM VELOUTÉ

This soup has a velvety texture that showcases the true flavours of the mushrooms. I use a hand blender with excellent results. This also eliminates the fuss of transferring hot soup to a conventional blender. Any type of mushroom works, even the humble button or field mushroom. The sour cream topping adds elegance and richness. It is optional but a wonderful treat now and again.

Heat a large soup pot over medium-high. Add the oil and onions and sauté until the onions soften and just begin to brown. Add the dried and fresh mushrooms and continue to cook until all moisture is evaporated. Add the potato, celery, and garlic. Sauté until the vegetables soften, about 5 minutes.

Add the stock and bring the soup to a boil. Add the rosemary, sage, and thyme and simmer until the potatoes are tender, about 10 minutes. Purée the soup with a hand blender until very smooth. You may have to purée the soup a couple of times to make it very velvety. (You can also purée the soup in a blender.)

Simmer the soup for 20–30 minutes, then add the whipping cream and bring back to a boil. Reduce the heat and season with salt and pepper. Meanwhile, in a mixing bowl, combine the sour cream, porcini powder, and balsamic vinegar. Whisk until smooth and set aside until needed. To serve, place a ladle of soup in a serving bowl and top with a spoonful of porcini cream. The cream will begin to melt and float on the surface. Garnish with minced chives and serve immediately.

1 Tbsp (15 mL) grapeseed oil
1 lb (454 g) spot prawns
1 tsp (5 mL) salt
1 tsp (5 mL) sugar
1 Tbsp (15 mL) grapeseed oil
1 large onion, peeled and chopped
2 large carrots, peeled and chopped
1 stalk celery, chopped
4 quarts (4 L) prawn or crab stock (p. 156)
4 slices fresh ginger
1 head garlic, peeled and chopped
1 bunch cilantro (stems and stalks)
juice and zest of 1 lime
1 can (14 oz [400 mL]) coconut milk
2 cups (500 mL) chopped fresh seaweed
salt and pepper, to taste
fresh cilantro leaves (or basil), for garnish

SERVES 6–8

THAI-FLAVOURED SPOT PRAWN AND SEAWEED BISQUE

Spring is the local season for our Pacific spot prawns. If you can buy them live, the heads make the most amazing stock. If they are not available, you can use crab shells to make a good substitute. The shells will keep in the freezer for up to 1 month before you use them.

Peel prawns (reserve shells) and place in a shallow metal or glass tray. Sprinkle lightly with salt and sugar. Cover with boiling water and let sit for 5 minutes. Drain and cool to room temperature. Peel prawns and chill until needed.

In a stockpot, add the oil as well as the onion, carrots, and celery. Sauté until they begin to brown, about 2–3 minutes. Add stock, ginger, garlic, cilantro, lime juice, lime zest, coconut milk, and seaweed. Bring to a boil, reduce the heat, and simmer for 30 minutes, or until the vegetables are tender.

Purée the soup with a hand blender until smooth. Check the seasoning and adjust with salt and pepper (or hot sauce if you like it spicy). To serve place the prawns in the serving bowls and ladle the hot soup overtop. Garnish with cilantro leaves and serve immediately.

1 cup (250 mL) diced onions

2 cups (500 mL) diced mushrooms
(chanterelle, lobster, morel, etc.)

2 cups (500 mL) diced burdock root

1 cup (250 mL) shredded carrot

1 cup (250 mL) diced celery

2 Tbsp (30 mL) minced garlic

4 quarts (4 L) mushroom vegetable
broth (p. 155) (or water)

4 cups (1 L) shredded cabbage

4 large potatoes, peeled and diced

2 cups (500 mL) diced cooked beets

½ cup (125 ml) fresh chopped dill

1 cup (250 mL) sour cream

2 green onions, finely minced

SERVES 6–8

BURDOCK AND MUSHROOM BORSCHT

Real borscht is one of the triumphs of home-style cooking. For best results, it must be made in big batches and savoured over a couple of days. The burdock adds immune-system-building nutrition and a fantastic nutty and chewy texture to the soup.

Heat a large soup pot over medium-high. Add the oil and onions and sauté until the onions soften and just begin to brown. Add the mushrooms and continue to cook until all moisture is evaporated. Add the burdock root, carrot, celery, and garlic. Sauté until the vegetables soften, about 5 minutes.

Add the broth and bring the soup to a boil. Add the cabbage, potatoes, and beets. Bring back to a simmer and cook until the potatoes are tender, about 10 minutes. Add the dill and stir to mix.

The soup is best when made a day in advance, cooled, and reheated to order. Garnish with a dollop of sour cream and a sprinkling of green onions.

PASTA & NOODLES

2 cups (500 mL) buckwheat flour
½ cup (125 mL) all-purpose flour
1 tsp (5 mL) salt
¾ cup (175 mL) water

MAKES 4 SERVINGS

SOBA NOODLES

Soba is made from buckwheat, a type of plant that is related to sorrel and rhubarb. Buckwheat is one of the earliest known crops seen in the historical record. You can make the pasta without any wheat but it makes it very difficult to handle, particularly for beginners. You can substitute tapioca flour or gluten-free flour mixes for the all-purpose flour.

In the bowl of a food processor, pulse together the buckwheat flour, all-purpose flour, and salt. Add the water and pulse to mix. Add additional water 1 tablespoon (15 mL) at a time if the mixture seems dry and crumbly. When enough water is added, the dough will come together in a ball. Remove from the food processor, wrap in plastic wrap, and refrigerate for at least 1 hour.

Cut the dough into 2 pieces and run each piece through a pasta machine to make long, thin sheets. Lay each sheet on a flat work surface. Cut the sheets into 1-foot (30 cm) segments and either cut with a knife (or pizza cutter) or use the pasta cutter attachment of the pasta machine to make linguini or spaghetti.

1 cup (250 mL) all-purpose flour
1 Tbsp (15 mL) seaweed powder (p. 20)
½ tsp (2 mL) salt
1 egg, beaten
2 Tbsp (30 mL) water

SERVES 4

SEAWEED-FLAVOURED PASTA

Seaweed adds great flavour and an essence the Japanese call *umami*—which translates to "savoury." Umami is considered one of the great building blocks of flavour. A food processor makes short work of the job of making this pasta. It is also good for making ravioli and lasagna. For a simple meal, boil the pasta and toss it with a little butter, olive oil, and Parmesan cheese.

In the bowl of a food processor, pulse together the flour, seaweed powder, and salt. Add the egg and pulse again to mix. Add the water 1 tablespoon (15 mL) at a time until the dough comes together in a ball. Remove from the food processor, wrap in plastic wrap, and refrigerate for at least 1 hour.

Cut the dough into 2 pieces and run each piece through a pasta machine to make a long, thin sheet. Lay each sheet on a flat work surface.

Cut the sheets into 1-foot (30 cm) segments. These can be cooked and used as pasta sheets for lasagna or ravioli. You can also cut the sheets with a knife (or pizza cutter) or use the pasta cutter attachment of the pasta machine to make pappardelle, linguini, or spaghetti.

Cook the pasta in boiling salted water for 3–4 minutes, then drain and serve with butter, olive oil, or chanterelle tomato sauce (p. 183).

Variation:
1 Tbsp (15 mL) mushroom powder (p. 19) in place of the seaweed powder

Jelly
1 cup (250 mL) apple cider
¼ cup (60 mL) dried seaweed
1 tsp (5 mL) sesame oil
1 Tbsp (15 mL) cider vinegar
12 beach oysters, chopped
1 Tbsp (30 mL) agar-agar

1 recipe fresh soba noodles (p. 167)
1 small seedless cucumber, julienned
1 Tbsp (15 mL) toasted sesame seeds

SERVES 4

SOBA NOODLES WITH OYSTER AND SEAWEED JELLY

Soba is traditionally served chilled with a vinegar-and-soy-based sauce. This recipe uses an oyster and seaweed jelly to create a fantastic textural contrast. You can cook the soba ahead of time, cool, and place on a baking sheet lined with parchment paper. Chill and toss the noodles to separate the strands. A light drizzle of oil will keep them from sticking. If you are going to do this, it is a good idea to slightly undercook the noodles as they will absorb moisture as they sit.

Heat a large saucepan over medium and add the cider, seaweed, sesame oil, and cider vinegar. Bring to a boil and add the chopped oysters. Reduce the heat to a simmer and poach for about 2–3 minutes, or until the oysters are firm and cooked through. Add the agar-agar and stir to dissolve and mix in. Transfer to a storage container and cool to room temperature. When cool, transfer to the refrigerator and chill for at least 2 hours.

Heat a saucepan filled with salted water over medium-high. Add the noodles and reduce the heat to a simmer when the pot begins to foam. Stir occasionally to separate the noodles. Cook until the noodles are al dente, about 5–6 minutes. Drain noodles and shake to expel excess moisture. Let the noodles cool down slightly, tossing occasionally to separate the strands. At this point, the noodles can be drizzled with vegetable oil and placed on a tray to cool to room temperature.

To serve, transfer the noodles to a serving bowl, top with the oyster jelly, cucumber, and sesame seeds. Serve immediately. Each diner will toss the noodles to mix before eating.

1 lb (454 g) spaghettini pasta

2 Tbsp (30 mL) butter

1 Tbsp (15 mL) minced fresh garlic

2 cups (500 mL) chopped mushrooms (chanterelle, oyster, porcini, etc.)

1 Tbsp (15 ml) minced fresh sage

2 cups (500 mL) chopped wild greens (lamb's quarters, sheep sorrel, oxeye daisy, etc.)

2 Tbsp (30 mL) extra-virgin olive oil

salt and pepper, to taste

2 Tbsp (30 mL) freshly grated Parmesan cheese

additional freshly grated Parmesan cheese, for garnish

extra-virgin olive oil, for garnish

SERVES 4

SPAGHETTINI WITH WILD GREENS AND MUSHROOMS

Sometimes the simplest recipes are the best ones. This is a quick and easy dish that creates spectacular results. In the spring, I use wild oyster mushrooms and fresh wild greens. In the fall, I often use chanterelles and wild mustard or kale from the garden. Try to find the thinner spaghettini noodles (or angel hair pasta), good Parmesan cheese, and the best possible olive oil.

Heat a pot of salted water over medium-high. When boiling, add the spaghettini pasta and cook until al dente (about 7–8 minutes). Reduce the heat and add a little oil if the pot foams excessively. When cooked, drain into a colander and toss with a little oil to prevent the noodles from sticking together.

Heat a sauté pan over medium and add the butter, garlic, and mushrooms. Cook until the mushrooms give off moisture and eventually appear dry. Add the sage and the chopped greens. Toss to wilt the greens and evaporate any moisture that appears.

Add the cooked pasta and toss to coat. Add the olive oil and season well with salt and pepper. At the last minute, toss in the grated cheese and toss to mix. Serve immediately with a little extra cheese grated on top and a drizzle of good olive oil.

1 lb (454 g) seaweed-flavoured pasta sheets (p. 168) or lasagna noodles
vegetable oil, for coating
2 Tbsp (30 mL) butter
24 beach oysters, shucked
1 cup (250 mL) dried seaweed
2 cups (500 mL) spinach
1 recipe seaweed béchamel sauce (p. 182)
2 cups (500 mL) shredded mozzarella cheese

SERVES 6

OYSTER AND SEAWEED LASAGNA

This dish tastes like the ocean. It is equally good with the seaweed pasta or with plain pasta. The dish can be assembled ahead and chilled, or frozen uncooked for up to 1 month. Thaw in the refrigerator for several hours (or overnight) and bake according to instructions.

Heat a pot of salted water over medium-high. When boiling, add the noodles and cook until al dente (about 8 minutes). Reduce the heat and add a little oil if the pot foams excessively. When cooked, drain into a colander and toss with a little oil to prevent the sheets from sticking together.

Heat a sauté pan over medium and add the butter and oysters. Cook for 1–2 minutes to firm up the oysters. Add the seaweed and spinach and toss to coat. Set aside to cool slightly.

Preheat the oven to 350°F (180°C).

In a casserole dish, add a spoonful of the béchamel sauce, top with a layer of cooked pasta sheets. Add a third of the oyster mixture and a light sprinkling of cheese. Repeat with the remaining layers of lasagna (keep about 1 cup [250 mL] of cheese for the top layer).

Place the lasagna in the oven and bake for 30 minutes, or until the top is golden brown and bubbling. Serve warm. (Can be made in advance and reheated.)

1 cup (250 mL) hazelnuts
1 lb (454 g) dry linguine pasta
2 Tbsp (30 mL) extra-virgin olive oil
1 Tbsp (15 mL) minced fresh garlic
½ cup (125 mL) stinging nettle pesto (p. 74)
2 Tbsp (30 mL) freshly grated Parmesan cheese (optional)
freshly grated Parmesan cheese, for garnish
extra-virgin olive oil, for garnish

SERVES 4

LINGUINE WITH HAZELNUTS AND STINGING NETTLE PESTO

This is another simple pasta that works magic with nettles and roasted hazelnuts. Make sure you keep a close eye on the hazelnuts as they are very easy to burn; a little browning is actually good, but too much will bring a bitterness to the final product. This is a rich and satisfying pasta.

Preheat the oven to 350°F (180°C). Place hazelnuts on a baking tray and place in the oven. Roast until the nuts start to brown, 5–7 minutes. Remove the tray from the oven and place the nuts in a clean kitchen towel. Bunch the towel around the nuts to form a tight ball. Grasp the ends of the towel and gently roll the ball on the work surface. This helps to loosen the skins of the hazelnuts. Open the towel and pick out the nuts that have shed their skin, repeat again to help remove any skins that remain. Depending on the freshness of the nuts, it may be difficult to remove all the skins; don't worry, just remove as much as you can. Transfer the nuts to a cutting board and chop finely. Set aside until needed.

Heat a pot of salted water over medium-high. When boiling, add the linguine pasta and cook until al dente (about 8–9 minutes). If the pot foams excessively, reduce the heat and add a little oil. When cooked, drain the linguine into a colander and toss with a little oil to prevent the pasta from sticking together.

Heat a sauté pan over medium and add the olive oil, hazelnuts, and garlic. Stir to coat the nuts in oil. Add the pesto and a few spoonfuls of water to dilute the pesto slightly. Add the cooked pasta; toss to coat and season well with salt and pepper. If using Parmesan cheese, add it at the last minute and toss to mix. Serve immediately with a little cheese grated on top and a drizzle of good olive oil.

2 lb (about 1 kg) Manila clams
1 Tbsp (15 mL) grapeseed oil
1 Tbsp (15 mL) minced fresh ginger
1 Tbsp (15 mL) minced fresh garlic
2 Tbsp (30 mL) fermented black
  beans (or bean sauce)
1 red pepper, cored and chopped
1 small onion, peeled and chopped
1 small red chili, seeded and minced

1 Tbsp (15 mL) honey
1 cup (250 mL) clam juice
  (from cooking)
1 Tbsp (15 mL) tapioca flour
1 tsp (5 mL) sesame oil
¼ cup (60 mL) chopped fresh
  cilantro
1 lb (454 g) fresh rice noodles

SERVES 4

RICE NOODLES WITH CLAMS AND BLACK BEAN SAUCE

Fresh rice noodles are becoming increasingly available. If you can't find them, you can substitute dried rice noodles; look for the thick noodles you would use in Pad Thai. Soak the noodles in hot water for 15 minutes before proceeding with the recipe.

Heat a large saucepan over medium and add about ¼ cup (60 mL) water. Toss in the clams and bring to a boil. Stir clams and remove clams as they open, placing them in a mixing bowl. Repeat until all the clams have opened. After 5 minutes of cooking, discard any clams that have not opened. Reserve 1 cup (250 mL) of the clam cooking juice; discard the remainder (including any sediment on the bottom).

Heat a non-stick skillet over medium-high. Add the oil, ginger, garlic, and black beans. Sauté for 1 minute, until fragrant but not burning. Add the pepper, onion, and chili. Sauté for an additional minute. Add the honey and allow to melt, then quickly add the clam juice and stir to mix. Bring back to a boil. Mix the tapioca flour with an equal amount of cold water; stir until dissolved. Pour the mixture into the boiling sauce and stir to mix well. Add the sesame oil and cilantro and set aside until needed.

Place the fresh rice noodles in a bowl and cover with boiling water. Let sit for 1–2 minutes. Drain the noodles and immediately add to the hot black bean sauce along with the clams. Stir to mix and transfer immediately to a serving plate. Serve warm.

1 lb (454 g) fresh chow mein noodles

1 Tbsp (15 mL) grapeseed oil

1 lb (454 g) ground pork

1 tsp (5 mL) five-spice powder

1 Tbsp (15 mL) minced fresh garlic

1 small onion, peeled and diced

1 Tbsp (15 mL) tapioca flour (or cornstarch)

1 cup (250 mL) chicken stock (or water)

2 Tbsp (30 mL) hoisin sauce

1 tsp (5 mL) hot sauce (or to taste)

1 tsp (5 mL) sesame oil

2 cups (500 mL) chopped wild mustard leaves (or oxeye daisy, dandelion, etc.)

1 cup (250 mL) fresh bean sprouts

SERVES 4–6

CHOW MEIN WITH MINCED PORK, WILD MUSTARD, AND HOISIN SAUCE

This is a crispy chow mein that benefits from a brief roasting in the oven. The result is a crispy chow mein cake that is crunchy on the outside and soft inside. The strongly flavoured sauce works with almost any type of edible wild greens.

Preheat the oven to 350°F (180°C).

Heat a large saucepan of water over high and add the noodles. Cook until the noodles soften and become tender, about 2–3 minutes. Drain noodles into a colander. Heat a non-stick skillet over medium-high and add the grapeseed oil. Add the noodles and cook until the bottom of the noodles begins to brown. Flip over the noodles and brown the underside of the noodles, another 2–3 minutes. Transfer the noodles to a baking tray and place in the oven. Bake for 5–10 minutes while you make the sauce.

Heat a clean, non-stick skillet over medium-high. Add the ground pork, five-spice powder, garlic, and onion. Sauté until the pork begins to brown and is cooked through. Sprinkle on the tapioca flour and stir into the meat. Add the chicken stock and stir to mix. Add the hoisin sauce, hot sauce, and sesame oil. Stir and cook until the mixture thickens. Just before serving, add the mustard leaves and bean sprouts and stir to coat with sauce.

Remove the noodles from the oven and place on a serving plate. Top with the pork sauce and serve warm.

CHANTERELLE BUTTONS

SAUCES

2 Tbsp (30 mL) butter
2 Tbsp (30 mL) flour
1 Tbsp (15 mL) wild mushroom powder (porcini, oyster, bolete, etc.) (p. 19)
2 cups (500 mL) milk (or half milk and half stock)
salt and pepper, to taste

MAKES ABOUT 2 CUPS (500 ML)

WILD MUSHROOM BÉCHAMEL SAUCE

This variation can be used as the base for a great pasta (like mushroom mac and cheese) or used as a sauce for pizza and flatbread.

In a saucepan over medium-high heat, add the butter. Heat until sizzling, then add the flour and whisk until smooth. Add the mushroom powder and stir to mix. Add the milk and whisk until smooth. Cook for 10 minutes over low heat until smooth and thick. Season well with salt and pepper. Serve as a sauce for pasta or vegetables, or use as the base in several recipes in this book.

2 Tbsp (30 mL) butter
2 Tbsp (30 mL) flour
1 Tbsp (15 mL) seaweed powder (p. 20)
2 cups (500 mL) milk (or half milk and half stock)
salt and pepper, to taste

MAKES ABOUT 2 CUPS (500 ML)

SEAWEED BÉCHAMEL SAUCE

Béchamel is another mother sauce that can be used in a number of preparations. The sauce will thicken as it sits. Thin with additional milk if necessary to achieve a pourable consistency. You can also make a wheat-free version using rice flour or tapioca flour.

In a saucepan over medium-high heat, add the butter. Heat until sizzling, then add the flour and whisk until smooth. Add the seaweed powder and stir to mix. Add the milk and whisk until smooth. Cook for 10 minutes over low heat until smooth and thick. Season well with salt and pepper. Serve as a sauce for pasta or vegetables, or use as the base in several recipes in this book.

2 Tbsp (30 mL) extra-virgin olive oil
4 cups (1 L) fresh chanterelles
1 large onion, chopped
1 large carrot, peeled and chopped
1 large stalk celery, diced
1 Tbsp (15 mL) minced fresh garlic
8 cups (2 L) stewed tomatoes
2 bay leaves
1 Tbsp (15 mL) chopped fresh sage
2 Tbsp (30 mL) chopped fresh marjoram
1 tsp (5 mL) hot sauce
1 tsp (5 mL) honey
salt and pepper, to taste

MAKES ABOUT 10 CUPS (2.5 L)

CHANTERELLE TOMATO SAUCE

This sauce is an excellent way to preserve a harvest of chanterelles. It also works well with oyster mushrooms and porcini if you are really lucky in your foraging. The sauce is great for pasta and pizza and as an all-purpose tomato sauce.

In a large stockpot, add the olive oil and chanterelles. Heat until the mushrooms give off moisture and it is evaporated. Add the onion, carrot, celery, and garlic, stirring until the mixture browns and just begins to stick to the bottom of the pan. Add the tomatoes and stir well to mix. Reduce the heat to a simmer and add the bay leaves, sage, and marjoram. Stir to mix and then season with hot sauce, honey, salt, and pepper.

Simmer for 1 hour, stirring occasionally. Remove from the heat and allow to cool to room temperature. Remove the bay leaves. The sauce can be refrigerated for 3–4 days or can be frozen for up to 1 month. Transfer to zip-lock bags and freeze flat on a cookie tray. When frozen, stack bags to store in the freezer.

1 cup (250 mL) white wine
¼ cup (60 mL) minced shallots
1 Tbsp (15 mL) minced fresh tarragon (optional)
1 cup (250 mL) fresh sheep sorrel leaves
¼ cup (60 mL) water
1 tsp (5 mL) prepared mustard
¼ cup (60 mL) butter, chilled and cubed
salt and pepper, to taste

MAKES ABOUT ½ CUP (125 ML)

SHEEP SORREL BUTTER SAUCE

This sauce is great with any type of fish. It is a classic match with salmon but is also wonderful with halibut and trout. The sauce is also a great pairing with cooked asparagus, broccoli, or cauliflower.

In a saucepan over medium, heat the wine, shallots, and tarragon (if using). Reduce until most of the liquid has evaporated—2 tablespoons (30 mL) should remain. Remove from the heat and set aside until needed.

Heat a clean saucepan of salted water over high until boiling. Add the sorrel and blanch for 1–2 minutes. Drain and add to the reduced wine. Add the water and mustard and purée with a hand blender (or table-top blender), then return to the pan. Bring to a boil, remove from the heat, and add the butter cubes to the pan. Whisk or swirl pan until the butter melts, thickening the sauce. Taste and season with salt and pepper. Keep sauce warm and do not reheat the sauce.

4 cups (1 L) water
1 cup (250 mL) chopped fresh seaweed (or ½ cup [125 mL] crumbled dried seaweed)
1 Tbsp (15 mL) miso paste
1 Tbsp (15 mL) soy sauce
2 Tbsp (30 mL) mirin (or 1 Tbsp [15 mL] honey)
1 tsp (5 mL) hot sauce
1 tsp (5 mL) sesame oil

MAKES ABOUT 4 CUPS (1 L)

ASIAN SEAWEED SAUCE

Seaweed makes a versatile sauce that freezes well. When I get a batch of fresh seaweed, I often make this sauce and store it in 1-cup (250 mL) containers. It is great in stir-fries or added to soups and chowder for intense flavour and lots of health-promoting nutrients. Use fresh or dried seaweed with great results.

Heat a saucepan over medium-high and add the water and seaweed. Bring to a boil, reduce to a simmer, and add the miso, soy, mirin, hot sauce, and sesame oil. Simmer for 10 minutes, at which point the seaweed should be completely soft. Purée with a hand blender until a smooth sauce is produced.

Transfer to a storage container and cool to room temperature. Can be kept in the refrigerator for 3–4 days, or frozen for up to 1 month.

1 Tbsp (15 mL) vegetable oil
2 onions, peeled and diced
2 cups (500 mL) minced mushrooms (oyster, chanterelle, button, etc.)
2 Tbsp (30 mL) porcini powder (p. 19)
2 Tbsp (30 mL) minced fresh garlic
2 Tbsp (30 mL) minced fresh sage
2 Tbsp (30 mL) minced fresh rosemary
1 cup (250 mL) beer
½ cup (125 mL) tomato paste
2 cups (500 mL) stewed tomatoes
¼ cup (60 mL) bigleaf maple syrup
½ cup (125 mL) cider vinegar
1 Tbsp (15 mL) hot sauce (or more to taste)
½ cup (125 mL) molasses
salt and pepper, to taste

MAKES ABOUT 4 CUPS (1 L)

MAPLE AND MUSHROOM BBQ SAUCE

This sauce will enliven ribs, chicken, or pulled pork. I've also used it successfully on grilled salmon and octopus. You can adjust the level of heat by using hot sauce or puréeing a hot pepper or two into the mix.

Heat a saucepan over medium-high and add the oil, onions, and mushrooms. Sauté until the mushrooms give off moisture and the mixture begins to stick to the bottom of the pan. Add the porcini powder, garlic, sage, and rosemary to the pan. Stir to mix and add in the beer. Stir to mix and cook until the beer is almost evaporated.

Add the tomato paste, stewed tomatoes, maple syrup, cider vinegar, hot sauce, and molasses. Reduce the heat and simmer for 30 minutes, stirring occasionally. Purée the sauce with an immersion blender until very smooth. Season with salt and pepper. Cool and transfer to a storage container.

Can be stored in the refrigerator for several weeks.

½ cup (125 mL) miner's lettuce or oxeye daisy tops
3 Tbsp (45 mL) diced white onion
1 Tbsp (15 mL) capers, rinsed and coarsely chopped
salt and pepper, to taste
2 Tbsp (30 mL) sherry vinegar
2 Tbsp (30 mL) fruity Spanish olive oil

MAKES ABOUT 1 CUP (250 ML)

WILD SALSA VERDE

This salsa is deep green and makes a wonderful compliment to grilled beef and lamb. The best greens to use are the milder ones like miner's lettuce and oxeye daisy. Purslane, sheep sorrel, and peppercress also work well. It is also best fresh and tends to oxidize if left too long.

In a bowl, combine the wild greens, onion, and capers. Season with salt and pepper. Cover with the vinegar and olive oil and mix well. Allow to sit for at least 30 minutes. Salsa will keep for 2–3 days in the refrigerator.

MUSSELS

SHELLFISH

1 Tbsp (15 mL) finely minced grand fir needles
1 tsp (5 mL) prepared mustard
2 Tbsp (30 mL) white wine vinegar
1 tsp (5 mL) water
2 Tbsp (30 mL) grapeseed oil
1 green onion, finely minced
12 freshly shucked oysters

MAKES ENOUGH FOR 12 OYSTERS

GRAND FIR VINAIGRETTE FOR OYSTERS

The pine and citrus notes of the fir needles work magic with fresh oysters. You can make the dressing below, or you can use grand fir jelly (p. 81) and add a fresh squeeze of lemon or lime to balance the sweetness.

In a small bowl, combine the grand fir needles, mustard, vinegar, and water. Whisk to mix and then add the oil in a slow, steady stream. Add the green onion and stir to mix. Season with salt and pepper and set aside until needed.

To serve, spoon a little vinaigrette over each shucked oyster and enjoy!

4 cups (1 L) fresh spinach, trimmed
sea salt
1 tsp (5 mL) minced fresh garlic
zest and juice of ½ a lemon
1 tsp (5 mL) hot sauce
1 tsp (5 mL) maple syrup or honey
2 Tbsp (30 mL) extra-virgin olive oil
12 large beach oysters
¼ cup (60 mL) fresh goat cheese
black pepper, to taste

MAKES 12 OYSTERS

BBQ OYSTERS WITH SPINACH AND GOAT CHEESE

Buy the freshest oysters you can find, preferably from a store that keeps them in a chill tank. The rate of cooking will depend on the size of the oysters. Discard any unopened oysters before you grill. On the grill, oysters sometimes become sealed shut by evaporating juices. You have to open them to check to see if they are fresh (no odour and plump when cooked).

Heat a small pot of water over high until it boils. Add the spinach and salt. Cook for 1 minute, or until the spinach is wilted and bright green. Drain and rinse under cold water; squeeze to remove all moisture. Place in a food processor or blender. Purée to a paste and add the garlic, lemon zest, lemon juice, hot sauce, maple syrup, and olive oil. Purée until very smooth. Season with salt and pepper. Set aside until needed.

Preheat the barbecue to high. Place the oysters on the grill and close the lid. Heat for about 5 minutes before lifting the lid. Look for oysters that have opened. Transfer opened oysters to a baking tray and remove the top shells. Continue cooking the rest of the oysters. If they haven't opened after an additional 2–3 minutes of cooking, you may have to force them open.

When all of the oysters are cooked, spoon the spinach purée onto the oysters and top with crumbled goat cheese and black pepper. Return the oysters to the grill and warm through (1–2 minutes). Transfer to a serving platter and serve warm.

Pancakes
¼ cup (60 mL) all-purpose flour
1 tsp (5 mL) baking powder
salt and pepper, to taste
4 eggs
1 Tbsp (15 mL) soy sauce
1 tsp (5 mL) sesame oil
2 large shucked oysters and juice
1 leek, washed and thinly sliced
2 Tbsp (30 mL) chopped fresh
 cilantro
oil, for frying

Sauce
½ cup (125 mL) rice vinegar
1 tsp (5 mL) brown sugar
1 Tbsp (15 mL) soy sauce
2 slices fresh ginger, cut in thin
 strips
1 tsp (5 mL) hot sauce
bean sprouts and fresh cilantro,
 for garnish

MAKES ABOUT 12 PANCAKES

KOREAN-STYLE OYSTER AND LEEK PANCAKES

These pancakes are often eaten as an appetizer in Korean restaurants but they will also make a great lunch or dinner with a side salad. You can add other seafood and shellfish, such as mussels, shrimp, crab, or squid, to the pancakes with great results.

In a mixing bowl, combine the flour, baking powder, salt, and pepper. In a small bowl, beat the eggs, soy sauce, sesame oil, and the oyster liquid together. Whisk the egg mixture into the flour mixture. Coarsely chop the oysters and add to the batter along with the leek and cilantro. Fold gently to combine.

Heat a non-stick pan over medium-high. Add 1 tablespoon (15 mL) of oil to the pan. Spoon the batter into the skillet to make three 3-inch (7.5 cm) pancakes. Brown lightly on each side until the edges of the pancakes are crisp. Remove to a serving platter and keep warm. Repeat with the remaining batter, adding oil to the pan as needed.

To make the sauce, combine the rice vinegar, brown sugar, soy sauce, ginger, and hot sauce in a small bowl. To serve, place a pancake on a plate, top with fresh bean sprouts and a few sprigs of cilantro. Drizzle with the sauce and serve immediately.

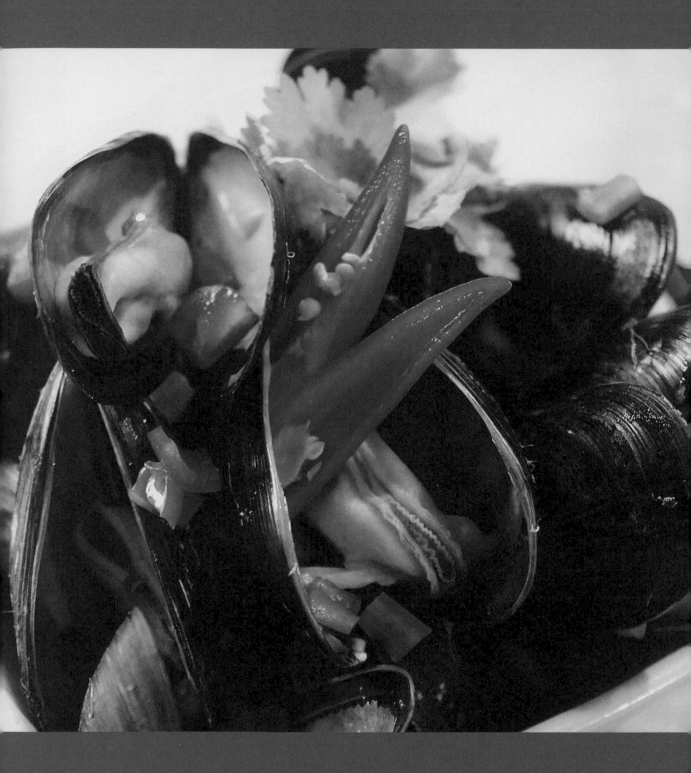

½ cup (125 mL) beer
1 Tbsp (15 mL) minced garlic
1 jalapeno pepper, seeded and minced
1 fresh tomato, cored and chopped
2 lb (about 1 kg) mussels
1 Tbsp (15 mL) chopped cilantro (or green onion)
1 Tbsp (15 mL) butter (or olive oil)

SERVES 4

MUSSELS STEAMED IN BEER, GARLIC, AND CHILIES

First buy mussels that are fresh from a store that knows good seafood. Just before cooking, look over the mussels and discard any that are opened and appear to be drying out. Remove any woolly beards that are attached to the shell. Don't do this too much in advance as it will kill the mussels. Place the mussels in a colander and quickly rinse. Immediately start the recipe below.

Heat a heavy-bottomed pot over medium-high and add the beer, garlic, jalapeno, and tomato. Bring to a boil and add the mussels. Cover with a lid and cook for 4–5 minutes, or until most of the shells have opened. Remove the lid and add the cilantro and butter. Stir to mix and cook for an additional 1–2 minutes.

Transfer to a large serving bowl and enjoy with fresh bread. Discard any mussels that didn't open.

2 lb (about 1 kg) mussels
¼ cup (60 mL) white wine
1 Tbsp (15 mL) grainy mustard
1 Tbsp (15 mL) maple syrup
1 Tbsp (15 mL) miso
1 Tbsp (15 mL) mayonnaise
¼ cup (60 mL) panko crumbs

SERVES 4–6

BAKED MUSSELS WITH A MAPLE, MUSTARD, AND MISO CRUST

Do not remove the mussel beards until just before cooking. Removing this thread will speed the decay of the mussels. The mussels can be steamed in advance and the dish assembled and chilled. To serve, warm the mussels under a broiler to brown the crust.

Place the mussels in a large bowl and rinse quickly with cold water. Pull off any threads attached to the side of the shell (the beards). Drain and set aside.

Place a large pot over medium-high heat. Add the wine and bring to a boil. Add the mussels and cover the pot with a lid; cook for 5 minutes, shaking the pot occasionally. When the mussels have just opened and are still plump, remove them from the pot and set aside. Reduce the juice over high heat until about 2 tablespoons (30 mL) of rich liquid is left (about 5 minutes).

Preheat the oven to broil.

In a small bowl, combine the mussel juice, mustard, maple syrup, miso, and mayonnaise to create a paste. Peel back the shell of a mussel (discard the top) and spread a little of the paste on top of the flesh. Sprinkle with breadcrumbs and place on a baking tray. Repeat with the remaining mussels. Place under the broiler until golden. Serve warm.

4 lb (about 2 kg) mussels
1 Tbsp (15 mL) butter (or oil)
1 green onion, sliced
1 Tbsp (15 mL) minced pickled ginger
1 Tbsp (15 mL) minced fresh garlic
¼ cup (60 mL) sake (or beer)
1 tsp (5 mL) wasabi paste
1 Tbsp (15 mL) light soy sauce
shredded nori, for garnish

SERVES 4

STEAMED MUSSELS WITH A SAKE-GINGER BROTH

The spicy and earthy flavours of Japan work well with mussels. If you want to add a spicier element, you can add hot sauce or a minced hot pepper to the broth. This dish is great served over steamed rice or with good bread to sop up the juices.

Place the mussels in a large bowl and rinse quickly with cold water. Pull off any threads attached to the sides of the shells (the beards). Drain the mussels and set aside.

Heat a large pot over medium-high. Add the butter, green onion, ginger, and garlic. When sizzling and fragrant, add the sake, wasabi, and soy sauce. Bring to a boil, add the mussels, and cook for 5 minutes, covering with a lid. Shake the pot occasionally. When the mussels have just opened and are still plump, transfer to a serving dish. Garnish with the shredded nori.

Serve hot with a warm French-style baguette to soak up the broth.

2 Tbsp (30 mL) light soy sauce
1 tsp (5 mL) minced ginger
1 Tbsp (15 mL) rice wine vinegar
1 tsp (5 mL) wasabi paste
1 tsp (5 mL) honey
1 fresh geoduck, sliced

SERVES 4

GEODUCK SASHIMI

This is the classic way to serve geoduck in Japan or Hong Kong. Fresh geoduck is essential for this dish. Geoduck clams are often shipped live to discriminating buyers in Asia. A whole geoduck should yield 24 slices, enough for 4 people.

In a small mixing bowl, combine the soy sauce, ginger, vinegar, wasabi, and honey. Allow to sit for at least 15 minutes.

Arrange the geoduck on a serving platter. With chopsticks, take each piece of geoduck and dip into the sauce (or pour over the entire platter). Serve immediately.

2 lb (about 1 kg) Manila clams
¼ cup (60 mL) dry white wine
1 Tbsp (15 mL) minced garlic

Vinaigrette
¼ cup (60 mL) chorizo sausage, finely chopped
4 Tbsp (60 mL) extra-virgin olive oil
1 Tbsp (15 mL) minced fresh flat-leaf parsley
2 Tbsp (30 mL) sherry vinegar
salt and pepper, to taste

SERVES 4

CHILLED WINE-POACHED CLAMS WITH CHORIZO VINAIGRETTE

This dish works better with larger clams. It is important to note, however, that sometimes these clams are a little tougher and take a little longer to open than smaller clams. The shellfish will give off lots of moisture, which tends to be salty. You will not have to add any additional salt to the recipe.

In a large, heavy-bottomed skillet, add the clams, wine, and garlic. Bring to a boil over high heat and cover with a lid, cook for 2–3 minutes, or until the majority of the clams begin to open. Large clams might take a little longer to open. You can remove the opened clams and transfer to a bowl. When all (or most) of the clams are opened, strain the liquid (reserve) and discard any unopened clams (these are probably dead). Allow to cool to room temperature. Cover and chill in the refrigerator until needed.

In a skillet, add the chorizo and olive oil. Heat over medium-high until the chorizo begins to cook and release oil. Transfer to a small bowl and allow to cool. Add the parsley, sherry vinegar, and season with salt and pepper.

Transfer clams to serving plates, removing the top half of the shells. Spoon the vinaigrette over the chilled clams and serve.

1 cup (250 mL) sliced geoduck
1 Tbsp (15 mL) tapioca flour
1 tsp (5 mL) potato starch
2 Tbsp (30 mL) grapeseed oil
1 tsp (5 mL) salt
1 Tbsp (15 mL) minced garlic paste
1 small red chili, seeded and minced
4 cups (1 L) sweet pea tips (or spinach)

SERVES 4

STIR-FRIED GEODUCK WITH GARLIC AND PEA TIPS

Geoduck and pea tips are another great combination. Be careful to stir-fry the geoduck only briefly, prolonged cooking will toughen the meat.

In a mixing bowl, combine the geoduck, tapioca flour, and potato starch; toss to mix. Immediately heat a non-stick skillet over medium-high. Add the oil and heat until almost smoking. Add the geoduck and stir-fry for 2–3 minutes or until the geoduck stiffens and just begins to brown.

Add the salt, garlic, and chili and toss to coat. Add the pea tips and quickly stir-fry until the greens just begin to wilt.

Transfer to a serving platter and serve immediately.

4 slices bacon, finely chopped

1 small onion, peeled and minced

1 Tbsp (15 mL) minced garlic

1 cup (250 mL) diced fresh porcini mushrooms

¼ cup (60 mL) light-bodied beer, white wine, or cider

¼ cup (60 mL) whipping cream

2 lb (about 1 kg) Manila clams

1 Tbsp (15 mL) minced flat-leaf parsley, for garnish

SERVES 4

STEAMED CLAMS WITH PORCINI AND BACON

This dish is amazing with porcini mushrooms but is also excellent with chanterelles or morels. Serve with slices of crusty bread.

In a skillet, add the bacon and render most of the fat. Add the onion, garlic, and mushrooms and sauté until the onions begin to brown. Add the beer or white wine and reduce the liquid by half. Add the cream and bring the mixture to a full boil. Reduce for 1–2 minutes, then add the clams and cover.

Cook until the clams open, about 4–5 minutes. Discard any clams that do not open. Sprinkle the minced parsley on top and serve immediately.

SPOT PRAWNS

FISH & CRUSTACEANS

2 lb (900 g) spot prawns
3 Tbsp (45 mL) rice flour
½ cup (125 mL) oil, for frying
2 Tbsp (30 mL) minced fresh garlic
1 small onion, peeled and finely diced
1 jalapeno pepper, chopped
2 Tbsp (30 mL) chopped fresh cilantro
salt and pepper, to taste

SERVES 4

WOK-FRIED CRISPY SPOT PRAWNS WITH GARLIC AND CHILIES

Spot prawns are in season for a short time and can be preserved by freezing in salt water. Run the prawns under cold water to defrost quickly. You can substitute side-stripe shrimp.

Peel the prawns and place in a small bowl. Sprinkle the rice flour on top and toss to coat. Place oil in a wok. Heat until very hot, then add the prawns individually. Stir with a large spoon or spatula. Have a metal bowl with a strainer off to the side. When the prawns are brown, about 1 minute, transfer to the sieve and pour off all but 1 tablespoon (15 mL) of oil.

Return the wok to the heat and add the garlic, onion, and jalapeno. Sauté until soft and beginning to brown. Add the prawns and cilantro and toss to coat. Season well with salt and pepper. Transfer to a plate and serve immediately.

2 lb (about 1 kg) side of wild salmon (sockeye, coho, etc.)
sea salt and pepper, to taste
2 Tbsp (30 mL) rosehip butter (p. 80) (or orange marmalade)
2 Tbsp (30 mL) grainy mustard
2 Tbsp (30 mL) minced fresh rosemary
juice of 1 lemon

SERVES 4–6

CEDAR-PLANKED SALMON WITH ROSEHIP BUTTER AND LEMON

Prepare a plank of cedar by giving it a good scrub with a brush and soaking it in a tub of water for at least 2 hours. Preheat a barbecue for at least 20 minutes. Salmon can also be baked in an oven with good (although less smoky) results.

Prepare the salmon by removing the pin bones and cutting the side into 1-inch (2.5 cm) strips, cutting down to, but not through, the skin of the fish. This will allow the marinade to penetrate and make serving the fish easier.

Preheat the barbecue to high.

On a baking tray, place the cedar plank and top with the salmon, skin side down. Season the salmon well with salt and pepper. In a small bowl, combine the rosehip butter, mustard, and rosemary. Stir to mix and allow the rosehip butter to dissolve. Drizzle the mixture over the salmon and spread over the fish's surface. Allow to sit for 15 minutes. Place the cedar plank on a hot BBQ grill and close the lid.

Cook for about 10 minutes. Lift lid and check doneness. You want the salmon to be moist and just starting to flake under light pressure. You will see beads of salmon fat begin to form on the cuts in the salmon. Remove from the heat and allow to rest for 5 minutes before serving. Drizzle with lemon juice and serve warm.

2 lb (about 1 kg) side of salmon (sockeye, Chinook, pink, or chum)
2 Tbsp (30 mL) honey
2 Tbsp (30 mL) sea salt
1 Tbsp (15 mL) cracked black pepper
¼ cup (60 mL) chopped fresh grand fir needles

SERVES 6–8

SMOKED SALMON WITH HONEY AND GRAND FIR NEEDLES

This is a variation on the traditional First Nations use of fir needles to cure salmon and smoke fish over pits of smouldering alder and maple wood. The effect is a unique combination of pine and citrus flavours. The honey helps to draw out moisture from the salmon and creates a denser flesh. I use a pellet smoker on the farm, but there are several inexpensive smokers available including the excellent Little Chief products.

On a cutting board, lay the salmon skin side down. Remove any pin bones and trim any fins or remains of bone. Make a small cut between the flesh and the skin. Holding the little bit of free skin, work the knife under the flesh. Slide the knife forward, removing the skin with as little flesh still attached as possible. Cut the salmon into 2-inch (5 cm) strips.

In a glass or stainless steel container, add the salmon, honey, sea salt, black pepper, and grand fir needles. Cover with plastic film and allow to sit for at least 30 minutes.

Heat the smoker, add soaked wood chips, and start to smoke the chips. Transfer the salmon to a rack, place in the smoker, and smoke for at least 30 minutes. Alternatively, you can use a cedar plank in a barbecue (see Chef's Tip). When cooking time has elapsed, test the salmon with a fork. It should just begin to flake under light pressure and small beads of fat will have formed on the surface of the fish. Serve warm.

Chef's Tip: To cook salmon on the barbecue, soak a piece of cedar in water for at least 1 hour. Preheat barbecue to high. Place the salmon on the cedar plank and add directly to the barbecue grill. Close cover and cook for at least 20 minutes.

4 smoked sablefish fillets (about 6 oz [170 g] each)

1 cup milk

1 Tbsp (15 mL) garlic

1 small onion, peeled and sliced

1 oz (28 g) small dried morel mushrooms

2 cups (500 mL) cherry tomatoes

1 cup (250 mL) white wine (or stock or water)

2 Tbsp (30 mL) minced fresh sage

1 tsp (5 mL) hot sauce

1 Tbsp (15 mL) butter

1 tsp (5 mL) fresh lemon zest

SERVES 4

SMOKED SABLEFISH BRAISED WITH MORELS AND TOMATO

Smoked sablefish (sometimes called black cod) is one of the treasures of the Pacific Northwest. It deserves a special sauce like this morel and tomato version. I use hothouse cherry tomatoes for sweetness and availability in the spring. This is a great dish to top risotto, soft polenta, pasta, or even mashed potatoes. Look for the natural smoked product, with a pale caramel colour made without artificial dyes (which tends to give the product a reddish hue)

Place sablefish fillets in a shallow container and add the milk, garlic, and onion. Cover with plastic wrap and refrigerate for at least 1 hour.

Place the morels in a heatproof bowl and cover with boiling water. Let sit for at least 15 minutes.

Preheat the oven to 350°F (180°C).

Heat an ovenproof sauté pan over medium-high and add the tomatoes, wine, sage, and hot sauce. Remove the sablefish from the milk mixture and strain out the onion and garlic. Reserve the fish and add the onion to the tomato mixture. Cook for 5 minutes or until the onion is soft. Purée with a hand blender, bring to a boil, and reduce the heat to a simmer.

Add the sablefish and simmer for 1–2 minutes. Transfer the pan to the oven for 10 minutes. Remove from the oven and transfer the fish to a serving plate. Whisk the butter and lemon zest into the tomato sauce. Check the seasoning and adjust with salt and pepper if necessary. Spoon the sauce over the fish and serve immediately.

Butter

2 cups (500 mL) whole oyster mushrooms

8 wild onions (or green onions)

1 Tbsp (15 mL) extra-virgin olive oil

salt and pepper, to taste

¼ cup (60 mL) butter

4 small trout (each about 1 lb [454 g]), head on

2 Tbsp (30 mL) extra-virgin olive oil

4 lemon wedges

SERVES 4

GRILLED TROUT STUFFED WITH WILD ONION AND OYSTER MUSHROOM BUTTER

Trout are one of the few farmed fish on the West Coast that are considered sustainable. Most trout available are rainbow and come to market at around 1 pound (454 g) per fish. You can cook them head on or remove the heads for the convenience of the diners. The butter can be made in advance and frozen for up to 1 month.

In a mixing bowl, combine the oyster mushrooms, onions, olive oil, salt, and pepper. Place the mushrooms and onions on a hot grill and cook until each side is charred and the mushrooms and onions are wilted. Transfer to a food processor and allow to cool slightly. Pulse until a coarse paste is formed. Add the butter and pulse until mixed. Remove from the processor and place the mixture on a sheet of plastic wrap. Fold over the plastic and form a compact log. Roll the log into the plastic film until it is well sealed. Grab the ends and twist in opposite directions until a compact and tight cylinder is achieved. Place in the refrigerator and chill for at least 30 minutes. Can be done well in advance.

Place trout on a small plate and drizzle with olive oil. Season well, inside and out, with salt and pepper. Place on a hot grill and cook about 3–4 minutes per side, or until the skin is charred and the flesh is cooked through. Gently remove from the grill and place on a serving plate. Allow to rest for 1–2 minutes. Remove the butter from the plastic film and cut into thick rounds. Place 2 rounds in each trout belly and serve immediately, with lemon wedges to drizzle juice overtop.

4 halibut fillets (about 6 oz [170 g] each)
1 Tbsp (15 mL) extra-virgin olive oil
1 Tbsp (15 mL) shredded fresh ginger
1 Tbsp (15 mL) brown sugar
1 Tbsp (15 mL) salt
1 tsp (5 mL) pepper
1 cup (250 mL) white wine
1 cup (250 mL) water
1 small onion, peeled and sliced
1 lemon, sliced
1 cup (250 mL) Asian seaweed sauce (p. 186)

SERVES 4

GINGER-POACHED HALIBUT WITH SEAWEED SAUCE

Poaching is a great way to handle lean fish like halibut. The marinade helps to lightly cure the fish and keep it moist and flaky. I use a microplane grater to render the ginger into a soft and fine shred.

Place halibut fillets on a plate and drizzle with olive oil, ginger, sugar, salt, and pepper. Cover with plastic wrap and refrigerate for at least 1 hour.

Heat a sauté pan over medium-high and add the white wine, water, onion, and lemon slices. Bring to a boil and then reduce the heat to a bare simmer. Add the halibut to the pan. Cover the pan and simmer for about 8–10 minutes. The halibut should be just firm to the touch if you poke it with your finger. Remove the fillets from the pan with a slotted spoon and let drain on a plate.

Meanwhile, in a small saucepan, heat the seaweed sauce to warm through. To plate, serve with rice and fresh spring vegetables like asparagus, Asian greens, or blanched stinging nettles. Serve warm.

4 ling cod fillets (about 6 oz [170 g] each)
1 tsp (5 mL) sesame oil
1 Tbsp (15 mL) minced fresh garlic
1 Tbsp (15 mL) salt
1 tsp (5 mL) pepper
½ cup (125 mL) stinging nettle pesto (p. 74)
2 cups (500 mL) water
2 slices ginger
1 lemon or lime, cut in wedges

SERVES 4

STEAMED LING COD WITH STINGING NETTLE PESTO

I like to serve this fish with a nice garden or wild foraged green salad. It also makes a great filling for fish tacos. The cod is tender and deliciously flaky. Any Pacific cod will work well, along with sablefish or halibut. I use a stainless steel steamer with pot bottom, perforated tray, and tight-fitting lid. You can also buy inexpensive bamboo steaming trays in Asian markets and at better cookware stores.

Place the ling cod on a plate and drizzle with the sesame oil, garlic, salt, and pepper. Turn to coat all sides. Spread the nettle pesto over the fish and turn again to coat all sides. Cover with plastic wrap and refrigerate for at least 1 hour.

Heat a large pot (fitted to the size of your steamer tray) with the water and slices of ginger. Place the fish on the steamer tray and place over the boiling water. Steam for 7–8 minutes, or until the fish is opaque and gently flakes to the touch. Remove from the pot and let sit on a plate for 1–2 minutes. Gently lift off with a spatula and place on serving plates. Serve with fresh greens and drizzle with fresh lemon or lime juice.

2 fresh Dungeness crabs (about 1½ lb [about 700 g] each)
4 Tbsp (60 mL) tapioca flour (or potato starch)
4 Tbsp (60 mL) canola oil
4 slices ginger, cut into a thin julienne
1 red chili, seeded and minced
2 Tbsp (30 mL) minced fresh garlic
2 Tbsp (30 mL) chopped fresh cilantro
2 green onions, minced
½ cup (125 mL) Asian seaweed sauce (p. 186)
salt and pepper, to taste

SERVES 4–6

STIR-FRIED CRAB WITH SPICY SEAWEED SAUCE

This recipe is best made with a wok to create that unique charring effect. You can also use a large non-stick skillet with good results. This is a messy dish that requires a crab cracker to open up the crab. The sauce is delicious and addictive. Serve with steamed rice and vegetables for a real treat.

Clean the crabs, remove their shells and guts, and rinse with cold water. Place the crabs flesh side up on a cutting board and cut each in half using a sharp, heavy knife. Cut between each leg to separate. Crack the legs (and thick points of shell) with the back of a knife to allow the seasoning to penetrate and make for easier eating. Place in a large bowl and dust with the tapioca flour. Toss the pieces to coat.

Immediately heat a wok over high heat and add the oil and ginger. Heat until almost smoking and add the crab legs and chili. Stir-fry the crab legs until they begin to brown, about 3–4 minutes. Add the garlic and stir to mix in and allow the garlic to cook for about 1 minute. Do not allow the garlic to burn. Add the chopped cilantro and green onions and toss to coat. Add the seaweed sauce and briefly toss (30 seconds) to warm through. Transfer to a serving platter and season with salt and pepper to taste. Serve warm with crab crackers, steamed rice, and vegetables.

1 lb (454 g) white fish (cod,
  halibut, sole)
¼ cup (60 mL) coconut milk
2 cups (500 mL) crab meat (from
  about a 1½ lb [700 g] crab)
1 tsp (5 mL) minced fresh garlic
1 tsp (5 mL) minced fresh ginger
1 cup (250 ml) shredded sui choy
  (Chinese cabbage)

2 Tbsp (30 mL) chopped fresh
  wild mint
2 Tbsp (30 mL) chopped fresh basil
2 green onions, thinly sliced
salt and pepper, to taste
1 cup (250 mL) panko crumbs (or
  breadcrumbs)
2 Tbsp (30 ml) canola oil

MAKES 8 CAKES

THAI CRAB CAKES WITH WILD MINT AND HAZELNUT SATAY SAUCE

These cakes are held together with a mousse made of white fish and coconut milk. This makes a very juicy cake with a fine texture. These cakes are best cooked the day they are made.

In a food processor, add the fish and pulse until a rough paste is formed. Add the coconut milk and process until a smooth paste is obtained. Transfer to a mixing bowl and add the crab meat (without any juice), garlic, ginger, sui choy, mint, basil, green onions, salt, and pepper. Mix until a smooth mixture is achieved. Cook a small sample to test for seasoning and adjust if needed.

Using an ice cream scoop (or a ¼ cup [60 mL] measure), take a scoop of the mixture and form it into a ball with your hands. Place in the panko crumbs and roll to coat evenly. Press the ball to form a cake and place on a tray lined with parchment (or silicone) paper. Repeat with remaining crab mixture.

Heat a non-stick skillet over medium-high and add the oil. Add the crab cakes (in batches if needed) and fry until golden brown on each side. Transfer to a warm oven to rest while you finish cooking the cakes. Serve warm with hazelnut satay sauce (see page opposite).

2 Tbsp (30 mL) hot water
2 Tbsp (30 mL) hazelnut butter
juice and zest of 1 lime
¼ cup (60 mL) coconut milk
1 Tbsp (15 mL) fish sauce
1 Tbsp (15 mL) sweet soy sauce
1 Tbsp (15 mL) chopped basil
1 tsp (5 mL) curry paste
hot sauce, to taste

MAKES ABOUT ½ CUP (125 ML)

HAZELNUT SATAY SAUCE

I am lucky to have an abundance of hazelnut trees on my property. Once harvested the nuts are dried and will keep for quite a few months in the shell. Once shelled, the nuts are best frozen to extend their shelf live for up to 6 months.

In a saucepan over medium heat, add the hot water and hazelnut butter; whisk until smooth. Add the lime juice and zest, coconut milk, fish sauce, sweet soy sauce, basil, and curry paste. Whisk until smooth and cook for 1–2 minutes until glossy and aromatic. Season to taste with hot sauce and remove from the heat. Allow to cool to room temperature. Set aside until needed.

2 cups (500 mL) sea beans
½ cup (125 mL) white wine vinegar
1 Tbsp (15 mL) pickling spice
2 Tbsp (30 mL) sugar
1 lb (454 g) albacore tuna loin
1 Tbsp (15 mL) soy sauce
1 Tbsp (15 mL) honey
1 tsp (5 mL) black pepper
1 Tbsp (15 mL) grapeseed oil
1 Tbsp (15 mL) red wine vinegar
  (or sherry vinegar)

1 tsp (5 mL) prepared yellow
  mustard
1 Tbsp (15 mL) chopped fresh basil
2 Tbsp (30 mL) extra-virgin olive oil
1 small seedless cucumber, diced
1 cup (250 mL) quartered cherry
  tomatoes
1 cup (250 mL) cubed feta cheese
1 orange or yellow pepper, seeded
  and diced
salt and pepper, to taste

SERVES 4

SEARED TUNA AND PICKLED SEA BEAN SALAD

Albacore tuna is pale in colour and sometimes referred to as white tuna. The flesh is fairly lean, except around the belly of the tuna. The fish is best cooked medium-rare, allowing it to retain moisture and a soft and delicious texture. The sea beans should be soaked in plenty of cold water prior to using.

Rinse the sea beans in cold, running water. Heat a saucepan over high and add the white wine vinegar, pickling spice, and sugar. Bring to a boil, add the sea beans, and remove from the heat. Stir occasionally while preparing tuna.

On a plate, place the albacore tuna loin and drizzle with soy sauce, honey, and black pepper. Roll tuna to coat all sides. Heat a non-stick skillet over medium-high and add the grapeseed oil and tuna. Sear on all sides, about 1–2 minutes each side. The tuna should slightly blacken from the soy sauce and honey. Transfer to a clean plate and allow to rest. The tuna should still be quite rare in the centre.

In a salad bowl, add the red wine vinegar, mustard, basil, and olive oil; whisk to blend. Add the cucumber, tomatoes, feta, and pepper to the bowl. Using a pair of tongs, remove the sea beans from the pickle mix and add to the bowl. Toss to coat, taste, and adjust seasoning with salt and pepper. Cut the tuna loin into thick slices and place on top of the salad. Serve chilled or at room temperature.

MEAT & POULTRY

1 (2-inch [5 cm]) cut beef rib-eye
  steak (about 2 lb [1 kg])
2 Tbsp (30 mL) extra-virgin olive oil
1 Tbsp (15 mL) minced fresh garlic
1 Tbsp (15 mL) minced fresh
  rosemary
1 Tbsp (15 mL) porcini powder
  (p. 19)
1 tsp (5 mL) coarse sea salt
1 tsp (5 mL) black pepper
1 Tbsp (15 mL) butter

1 large onion, peeled and diced
1 carrot, peeled and diced
1 stalk celery, diced
1 cup (250 mL) sliced porcini
  mushrooms (or chanterelles or
  button mushrooms)
2 Tbsp (30 mL) all-purpose flour
2 cups (500 mL) beef, mushroom,
  or chicken stock

SERVES 4

CAST-IRON ROASTED PORCINI RIB-EYE STEAK

Old-school cast-iron pans evenly distribute heat and here create a thick crust of caramelized mushrooms and natural sugars. If you do not have one of these skillets, use a non-stick pan and finish the steak on a baking tray in the oven.

Place the steak on a large platter and drizzle with olive oil. Season with garlic, rosemary, porcini powder, sea salt, and black pepper. Spread the seasoning over the surface of the meat and rub in with your hands. Cover the steak with plastic film and set aside on the counter for 20 minutes.

Preheat the oven to 350°F (180°C).

Heat a cast-iron skillet over medium and add the butter. Add the meat and sear on both sides until lightly browned, about 5 minutes per side. Remove the steak from the pan and rest on a plate. Add the onion, carrot, and celery to the pan and toss to coat. Return the steak to the pan and place on top of the vegetables. Place the pan in the oven for 30 minutes or until a meat thermometer reads 120°F (50°C) for rare, 130°F (55°C) for medium-rare, 140°F (60°C) for medium, or 155°F (70°C) for well done. Remove the skillet from the oven, cover the steak with aluminum foil, and let rest for 15 minutes.

Meanwhile, return the skillet to the stove over medium heat. Add the porcini mushrooms and sauté for 2–3 minutes or until the mushrooms begin to brown. Add the flour and whisk to mix; heat until the flour begins to thicken. Add the stock and whisk until the mixture comes to a boil. Reduce the heat and stir occasionally for 10 minutes. Add any juices that have accumulated under the resting roast. Stir to mix. Check seasoning and adjust with salt and pepper if necessary.

Transfer the steak to a cutting board and cut on a diagonal into thick slices. Serve with porcini sauce on the side.

1 whole flank steak (about 2 lb [1 kg])
1 Tbsp (15 mL) prepared yellow mustard
¼ cup (60 mL) wild mushroom rub (see page opposite)
vegetable oil, for grill
salt and pepper, to taste

SERVES 4–6

GRILLED FLANK STEAK WITH A WILD MUSHROOM RUB

Flank steak is a relatively inexpensive cut that can be surprisingly tender when cooked to medium-rare. The mushroom rub is best left on overnight to allow the spices to penetrate the meat.

Place the flank steak on a platter and coat with the yellow mustard. Generously sprinkle with the spice rub. Cover with plastic wrap and refrigerate overnight.

The next day, remove from the refrigerator and allow to warm to room temperature for 30 minutes while you preheat the barbecue to high.

Clean the grill, then wipe with a paper towel drizzled with vegetable oil. Place the steak on the grill and reduce the heat to medium (or place the meat off to the side, away from the coals). Cover the barbecue and cook the steak for 15 minutes per side. Internal temperature should be 130°F (55°C) for medium-rare. Remove from the heat and place on a clean platter. Cover with aluminum foil and allow to rest for 10 minutes.

Transfer to a cutting board and carve the steak on a diagonal into thin slices. Season lightly with salt and pepper and serve warm.

1 cup (250 mL) mushroom powder (porcini, oyster, field, etc.) (p. 19)
¼ cup (60 mL) sugar
2 Tbsp (30 mL) salt
1 Tbsp (15 mL) chili powder
1 Tbsp (15 mL) ground black pepper
1 Tbsp (15 mL) garlic powder (not garlic salt)
1 Tbsp (15 mL) onion powder
1 Tbsp (15 mL) ground coriander
1 Tbsp (15 mL) ground cumin
1 Tbsp (15 mL) hot smoked paprika

MAKES ABOUT 2 CUPS (500 ML)

WILD MUSHROOM RUB

This is a versatile rub that works with chicken, pork, beef, lamb, and fish. After a few batches, you will probably want to double or triple the recipe. The rub stores well in a glass jar with a tight-fitting lid and will keep indefinitely.

In a mixing bowl, combine all the ingredients until evenly distributed. Set aside until needed. Store any extra in a glass jar with a tight-fitting lid.

4 whole lamb shanks (about 2 lb [1 kg])
1 head garlic, halved
4 medium leeks, split, washed, and trimmed
1 stalk celery, diced
2 carrots, peeled and diced
1 Tbsp (15 mL) minced fresh rosemary
1 Tbsp (15 mL) minced fresh sage
2 cups (500 mL) mushroom stock
2 cups (500 mL) apple cider
½ cup (125 mL) dried morel mushrooms

SERVES 4

BRAISED LAMB SHANK WITH MORELS, LEEKS, AND CIDER

Lamb shanks are another lower cost cut that transform into something wonderful when cooked for a long time in a flavourful braising liquid. The long cooking breaks down tough fibres in the meat and renders gelatin into the sauce. When properly cooked, the shank is fork-tender with a rich sauce that coats your tastebuds.

Preheat the oven to 350°F (180°F).

In a small roasting pan with a lid (or cover tightly in aluminum foil), place the lamb, garlic, leeks, celery, carrots, rosemary, sage, stock, and apple cider. Rinse the morels under hot water and drain. Add to the rest of the ingredients. Cover the pan and place in the oven for 1–1½ hours, or until the shanks are tender and easily pierced with a fork. Remove from the heat and allow to cool to room temperature. Transfer the entire mixture to a storage container and refrigerate overnight.

The next day, remove the fat layer from the top of the stock. Remove the lamb shanks and set aside. Place the liquid and vegetables into a large saucepan over high heat and reduce the volume by half.

Add the shanks back to the stock, reduce the heat, and simmer for 20 minutes or until the shanks are warmed through and very tender. Transfer to serving plates and serve with mashed potatoes, risotto, or soft polenta.

1 lb (454 g) pork shoulder
1 Tbsp (15 mL) rice flour (or tapioca flour)
1 Tbsp (15 mL) tapioca starch
1 Tbsp (15 mL) grapeseed oil
1 Tbsp (15 mL) minced fresh ginger
1 large onion, cut in wedges
1 chili, seeded and cut in thin strips
4 cups (1 L) wild greens (chickweed, oxeye daisy, nettles, etc.)
sesame oil, to season
salt and pepper, to season

SERVES 4

STIR-FRIED PORK WITH WILD GREENS AND GINGER

Stir-fries are a great way to get a meal on the table quickly. The secret is to have all of the ingredients ready before you start the brief process of cooking. The starch coating locks in all the juices and flavours. This leaves the pork slices very tender and makes them a perfect foil for the rich wild greens and chilies.

Place the pork on a cutting board and cut on a diagonal into thin slices. Transfer to a small bowl and add the rice flour and tapioca starch. Toss the pork to coat evenly. Immediately heat a non-stick skillet over high and add the grapeseed oil. Add the pork and stir-fry quickly until the pork begins to brown, about 3–4 minutes.

Add the ginger, onion, and chili to the skillet. Sauté until the onion just begins to soften and slightly char. Add the greens and stir-fry until wilted. Season with sesame oil, salt, and pepper. Transfer to a serving dish and serve warm.

1 deboned pork shoulder (about 4 lb [2 kg])
1 Tbsp (15 mL) minced garlic
1 cup (250 mL) apple cider
1 Tbsp (15 mL) extra-virgin olive oil
2 Tbsp (30 mL) salt
1 tsp (5 mL) freshly ground black pepper
1 cup (250 mL) grand fir needle tips, chopped

SERVES 6–8

SLOW-COOKED SALT AND GRAND FIR PORK SHOULDER

The grand fir adds an interesting and savoury element to this dish. Pork shoulder is often called Boston Butt or simply Butt Roast. It is a cut with a lot of fat and connective tissue and is perfect for roasting or slow grilling on the barbecue. I use a pellet smoker barbecue and a combination of oak and apple wood. The internal control thermometer should be set to 175°F (80°C).

Place the pork in a large container and rub the garlic into the meat. Pour the apple cider overtop of the pork. Cover the container with plastic wrap. Refrigerate overnight, turning occasionally.

The next day, remove the pork from the marinade and dry with a paper towel. Rub the skin side with olive oil and give the meat a good sprinkling of salt, pepper, and grand fir needles.

Turn on the burners on only one side of the barbecue (or bank the coals to one side of the grill) and place the meat on the unlit portion. This will give you indirect heat to cook the pork slowly.

Cook over a low temperature for about 2–3 hours, or until the internal temperature reaches about 155°F (70°C) (for well done). Remove the meat from the grill and cover with a piece of aluminum foil. Allow to sit for at least 15 minutes. Carve into thick slices and serve warm.

1 whole chicken (4 lb [about 2 kg])
1 Tbsp (15 mL) grapeseed oil
¼ cup (60 mL) curried mushroom rub (see page opposite)

SERVES 4

SPLIT ROASTED CHICKEN WITH CURRIED MUSHROOM RUB

Roasting chicken on the bone adds great flavour to the meat and makes the preparation of the meal easy—with spectacular results. This is a great dish for entertaining. The aroma of roasting chicken and curry spice will be a great motivator for your appetite.

Preheat the oven to 375°F (190°C).

Place the chicken on a cutting board, breast side down. With a serrated knife, cut down along the spine of the chicken, into the body cavity. Flip the chicken over and press down on the breast to flatten the bird.

Transfer to a roasting pan and drizzle with oil. Rub oil into the skin of the chicken. Flip over the chicken and sprinkle with curry rub. Flip the chicken again and sprinkle on the rest of the curry rub. Use your hands to work the rub into the skin of the bird.

Transfer to the oven and roast for 30–45 minutes, or until the skin is crispy and a thermometer into the leg reads 160°F (71°C).

Transfer to a platter, cover with aluminum foil, and allow to rest for 10 minutes. Chop the chicken into pieces (wings, legs, thighs, breast meat) and transfer to a serving platter. Serve warm.

1 cup (250 mL) mushroom powder (porcini, oyster, field, etc.) (p. 19)

¼ cup (60 mL) sugar

2 Tbsp (30 mL) salt

1 Tbsp (15 mL) ginger powder

2 Tbsp (30 mL) turmeric powder

1 Tbsp (15 mL) ground black pepper

1 Tbsp (15 mL) garlic powder (not garlic salt)

1 Tbsp (15 mL) onion powder

1 Tbsp (15 mL) ground coriander

1 Tbsp (15 mL) ground cumin

MAKES ABOUT 2 CUPS

CURRIED MUSHROOM RUB

The curry spices of the rub work well with chicken, pork, and beef. The mixture also works with roasted potatoes and cauliflower.

In a mixing bowl, combine all the ingredients until evenly distributed. Set aside until needed. Store any extra in a glass jar with a tight-fitting lid.

1 tsp (5 mL) minced fresh garlic
1 tsp (5 mL) salt
1 tsp (5 mL) ground black pepper
1 Tbsp (15 mL) light soy sauce
1 Tbsp (15 mL) maple syrup
1 tsp (5 mL) prepared yellow mustard
1 tsp (5 mL) sumac powder
4 quail (each about 4 oz [120 g])
vegetable oil, for grill

SERVES 4

GRILLED QUAIL MARINATED IN MAPLE, SOY, AND SUMAC

Sumac powder is made from the flower buds of the sumac tree and forms an acidic red spice. It is used extensively in the Middle East for its ability to brighten a dish. I collect the buds in the fall, dry them in the sun, and grind them to a fine powder. The spice will keep for up to a year if stored in a sealed jar.

In a small bowl, combine the garlic, salt, pepper, soy sauce, maple syrup, mustard, and sumac powder. Stir to mix. Place quail in a plastic zip-lock bag and add the marinade. Seal and shake the bag to distribute the seasoning. Place in the refrigerator overnight to allow flavours to penetrate the quail. Flip occasionally to redistribute the seasonings.

Preheat the grill to high. Preheat the oven to warm.

Clean the grill with a brush and rub with a paper towel drizzled with vegetable oil. Add the quail and cook for 3–4 minutes per side, or until the quail is slightly charred but still medium-rare. Transfer to a serving platter and place in the oven for 10 minutes to rest. Serve over salad greens or rice.

4 chicken legs (drumstick and thigh)
1 Tbsp (15 mL) garlic, minced
1 Tbsp (15 mL) minced rosemary
  (or sage)
salt and pepper, to taste

1 Tbsp (15 mL) butter
1 bunch green onions, minced
1 cup (250 mL) sliced fresh porcini
  mushrooms

SERVES 4

ROASTED BALLOTINE OF CHICKEN STUFFED WITH PORCINI MUSHROOMS

A ballotine is traditionally a roll of meat stuffed with filling. It is an excellent way to cook chicken, keeping the meat moist and allowing the skin to crisp up as the meat cooks. The ballotine can be made up to a day in advance and cooked in the oven or on the grill.

Place a chicken leg on a cutting board. Using your knife, slice down the inside of the drumstick and thigh and remove the bones. Repeat with the remaining legs. Rub the flesh with the garlic and rosemary. Season well with salt and pepper.

Heat a skillet over medium and add the butter. When sizzling, add the onion and mushrooms and cook until the mushrooms soften and give up their liquid. Remove from the heat and allow to cool.

Preheat the oven to 400°F (200°C).

Lay a piece of chicken skin side down on a cutting board. Place one quarter of the mushroom mixture down the middle of the flesh. Start at one end of the chicken piece and roll up the flesh into a log—with the skin on the outside of the roll. Cut a 12-inch (30 cm) section of butcher's twine. Wrap one end of the twine around one end of the log and tie snugly. Loop the remaining free length of twine around your fingers. Twist the loop and slide it under the chicken log. If you pull tightly on the end of the string, the loop should tighten around the chicken, pulling the flesh together in a tight log. Repeat looping the twine around the chicken until the log is tightly secured. Season chicken with salt and pepper. Alternatively, you can spray a piece of aluminum foil with oil and roll up the chicken log into a tight roll.

Sear the chicken in an ovenproof pan over high heat, then place the pan in the oven and roast the chicken for 30 minutes, or until a thermometer inserted into the log's centre reaches 160°F (71°C). Remove from the oven and allow the chicken to rest for 10 minutes before carving and serving.

To serve, cut the twine with a pair of scissors. With a sharp knife, cut the chicken into thin rounds. Place on a plate and serve with roasted potatoes, vegetables, and sauce. (I use a reduction of chicken stock with garlic and sage added at the last moment along with a teaspoon of cold butter. Swirl the pan until the butter melts, season with salt and pepper, and serve warm.)

DESSERTS

Crust

1 cup (250 mL) butter, melted
1 cup (250 mL) flour
1 cup (250 mL) oatmeal
1 cup (250 mL) brown sugar
1 cup (250 mL) ground hazelnuts
1 tsp (5 mL) vanilla

Filling

1 lb (454 g) cream cheese
½ cup (125 mL) bigleaf maple syrup
5 eggs
2 cups (500 mL) sour cream
1 tsp (5 mL) vanilla
1 tsp (5 mL) lemon juice

MAKES 8–12 PORTIONS

BIGLEAF MAPLE CHEESECAKE

The strong flavours of bigleaf maple syrup work well with the richness of cream. I have made several versions of this dessert over the years. One memorable experiment was to replace half the cream cheese with goat cheese. The tang of the goat cheese helped to balance the sweetness of the dessert. You can also make many variations by combining the cake with wild berry jam, jelly, or syrup.

Preheat the oven to 350°F (180°C).

In a large bowl, combine the melted butter, flour, oatmeal, sugar, hazelnuts, and vanilla. Stir well to mix and work with your hands until a crumbly mixture is formed. Press evenly into the sides and bottom of a 10-inch (25 cm) springform pan lined with parchment paper.

Place the cream cheese in a large bowl. Use an electric hand mixer on the lowest speed to beat the cream cheese until smooth. Add the maple syrup; add the eggs one at a time until incorporated. Add the sour cream, vanilla, and lemon juice. Beat at low speed until smooth and pour the filling onto the crust.

Bake for 45 minutes to 1 hour, then turn the oven off and leave the cake in the oven with the door open for a half hour. Transfer to a cooling rack and cool to room temperature. Cover with plastic wrap and refrigerate for at least 1 hour. Serve with your favourite wild berry jam or jelly, thinned with a little lemon juice to obtain a pouring consistency.

¾ cup (175 mL) sugar, divided
¼ cup (60 mL) water
1 tsp (5 mL) butter
2 cups (500 mL) whipping cream

1 cup (250 mL) mint leaves
4 large eggs
boiling water

MAKES 6 CUSTARDS

WILD MINT CRÈME CARAMEL

Crème caramel is one of the world's favourite desserts. I have made versions with several wild products including grand fir, sweet cicely, liquorice fern, and wildflower honey. All were delicious and most were eaten with no sounds being made—the sign that something wonderful is on the end of your spoon. One trick is to keep the oven temperature low and cook the custard until the edges set and the centre is still a little wobbly. The custard will continue to set up as it cools.

In a saucepan over high heat, combine a ¼ cup (60 mL) of the sugar with the water. Bring to a boil; reduce until the sugar begins to form large bubbles and begins to turn a light shade of golden brown on the edges. Add the butter and continue to cook until the butter has stopped foaming and the caramel is a nice golden brown (but not too dark or it will be bitter). The caramel will continue to cook in the pan so you must work quickly. Pour some of the caramel into 6 ramekins, covering the bottom of each one. Don't worry if there is leftover caramel in the pan.

Pour the cream into the saucepan that held the caramel. Add the mint and bring to a boil. Remove pan from the heat and let sit for 10 minutes.

Preheat the oven at 325°F (160°C).

Strain the mint from the cream. Return the pan with the cream to the stove, and bring to a simmer. Meanwhile, place the remaining ½ cup (125 mL) of sugar and the eggs in a mixing bowl; whisk until smooth. As soon as the cream reaches a boil, pour a third gently into the egg mixture, whisking constantly. Pour the remaining cream into the eggs and strain the custard into a clean bowl or pouring jug. Ladle or pour the custard mix into the ramekins.

Place the ramekins in an ovenproof pan and place the pan in the oven. Pour boiling water into the bottom of the pan, to cover half of the ramekin depth. Close the oven door and bake for 20–25 minutes, or until the custard is just set (it will still wobble gently in the centre when cooked). Transfer the ramekins to a cooling rack; cool to room temperature. Cover ramekins in plastic and chill until needed.

To serve, run a knife around the edge of each ramekin. Invert onto plates and gently shake until the custards slide out onto the plates.

1 portion (¼ of recipe) basic flaky pie dough (p. 90)
4 large eggs
1 cup bigleaf maple syrup (or medium or dark maple syrup)
1 cup (250 mL) milk
1 Tbsp (15 mL) tapioca flour
2 cups (500 mL) whipping cream
1 tsp (5 mL) vanilla extract

MAKES 8 SERVINGS

BIGLEAF MAPLE CUSTARD TART

Custard tarts are a wonderful expression of eggs and cream—and when combined with maple syrup, something amazing happens. Use a tart ring for this dessert. These are the tins with a removable outer ring and a solid metal base. This will allow you to lift the slices of pie without damaging the delicate crust and custard. This will make a 10-inch (25 cm) tart with a 2-inch (5 cm) rim.

Flour a cutting board and roll out the dough into a 12-inch (30 cm) circle. Fold the dough in half and place in a tart tray. Fold out the dough and gently ease it into the corners of the tray. Make sure to leave lots of slack in the dough along the sides. Roll a rolling pin across the top of the tart ring. This will trim the tart and allow the excess dough to fall around the edge. Press the dough on the inside of the tart so the pastry extends up above the edge of the tray. Prick the dough on the base of the tray with a fork and place in the refrigerator for at least 30 minutes.

Preheat the oven to 325°F (160°C).

Place a piece of aluminum foil in the interior of the tart tray, pressing down gently to the edges to cover the dough. Place in the oven and bake blind for 10–15 minutes, or until lightly browned. Remove from the oven and place on a cooling rack.

In a mixing bowl, add the eggs and maple syrup. Whisk to combine and set aside to let the foam settle down. In a small bowl, add the milk and tapioca flour. Whisk to combine and then pour the mixture into the eggs. Add the cream and vanilla and stir gently to mix.

Pour two-thirds of the filling into the pastry case. Slide the tart into the oven and pour in the remainder of the filling. Bake for 50–60 minutes, or until the custard firms but the centre of the tart is still slightly wobbly. Remove from the oven and place on a cooling rack until room temperature. Place in the refrigerator and chill for at least 1 hour. Run a knife around the outside of the shell to free the pastry and remove the outer ring of the tart tray. Cut into wedges and serve immediately.

1 cup (250 mL) milk
1 Tbsp (15 mL) powdered gelatin (or 2 tsp [10 mL] agar-agar powder)
2 cups (500 mL) whipping cream
1 vanilla bean (or 1 tsp [5 mL] vanilla extract)
¼ cup (60 mL) rosehip jelly
1 Tbsp (15 mL) honey
fresh fruit or berries, for serving

SERVES 4–6

ROSEHIP PANNA COTTA

I love Pacific Northwest rosehips. They are abundant and make a delicious edition to savoury and sweet products. This dish makes use of the sweet side of the rose and produces a shimmering dessert that is very easy to make. Gelatin produces the best results but agar-agar is a more appropriate choice if you have vegetarians in the house. Be sure to dissolve the agar-agar fully in the milk before proceeding with the recipe.

In a small saucepan over medium heat, add the milk and gelatin. Warm the milk and stir to dissolve the gelatin. Set the mixture aside for 5 minutes to steep.

In a large saucepan over high heat, add the whipping cream, vanilla, rosehip jelly, and honey. Bring to a boil, remove from the heat immediately, and add the gelatin mixture. Stir gently to mix. Test for sweetness, adding more honey to taste (if desired). Strain the mixture into a bowl, removing the vanilla bean.

Ladle the mixture into glass custard dishes that have been rubbed with a little oil (later helps to release the finished product). Place on a tray and cover with plastic wrap. Place in the refrigerator and chill for at least 2 hours (overnight is better).

Place the ramekins in warm water to loosen their contents, then invert onto serving plates. The panna cotta should slip from the glass. Give a gentle shake to release the vacuum (if needed) or dip back into the hot water to slightly melt the outer edge. Serve with fresh fruit or berries.

Crust

2 cups (500 mL) graham cracker crumbs

¼ cup (60 mL) melted butter

1 cup (250 mL) ground hazelnuts

½ cup (125 mL) brown sugar

¼ cup (60 mL) hazelnut butter

Filling

2 cups (500 mL) whipping cream

1 cup (250 mL) grand fir needle tips

¼ cup (60 mL) sugar

1 Tbsp (15 mL) Frangelico (hazelnut) liqueur

14 oz (420 g) dark chocolate, chopped

fresh berries, to garnish

icing sugar or cocoa powder, for dusting

MAKES 8–12 SERVINGS

GRAND FIR, CHOCOLATE, AND HAZELNUT TART

There is something magical about the combination of grand fir and chocolate, though spruce and pine tips would be just as pleasing. This dish is best made in the spring when the new growth tips of the trees are full of essential oil. Use the best dark chocolate you can find. I usually go for the ones with 70 percent cocoa solids from one of a number of new, small-scale producers.

In a mixing bowl, combine the graham cracker crumbs, melted butter, ground hazelnuts, and brown sugar. Heat the hazelnut butter in the microwave or in a hot water bath until smooth. Add to the crumbs and the mix will clump together when squeezed. Pour into a 12-inch (30 cm) tart pan (pastry cases with removable bases are best). Work the mixture into an even coating over the sides and bottom of the pan. Cover with plastic and chill or freeze until needed.

In a saucepan, add the whipping cream, grand fir needles, sugar, and Frangelico. Bring to a boil, remove from the heat, and pour through a strainer over the chopped chocolate. Stir until the mixture is smooth. Pour into the chilled tart shell. Allow to cool, then cover and chill in the refrigerator. To serve, cut into wedges and top with a mixture of fresh berries and a dusting of icing sugar or cocoa powder.

6 oz (170 g) dark chocolate
1 cup (250 mL) butter
2 cups (500 mL) sugar
4 eggs
1 cup (250 mL) flour
pinch salt
1 tsp (5 mL) vanilla
¼ cup (60 mL) crème de menthe (or 1 tsp [5 mL] mint extract)
1 cup (250 mL) fresh or frozen blackberries

SERVES 6–8

BLACKBERRY, MINT, AND CHOCOLATE CAKE

This will bring back childhood memories of the best brownie you have ever eaten. The cake is moist and chewy with the essence of blackberry and mint lurking at the centre. Go find the best dark chocolate available and enjoy the ride. You can use fresh or frozen blackberries for this cake. Raspberries and huckleberries also work well.

Butter a large 12-inch (30 cm) tart pan with a 2-inch (5 cm) rim (rim should be removable) and lightly dust with flour. Shake the flour around the pan to coat all the surfaces. Set aside until needed.

Preheat the oven to 350°F (180°C).

Combine the chocolate and butter and melt in a microwave for 1 minute. If still chunky, heat for 15 second intervals until just melted, then stir until smooth. You can also use a double boiler over hot water or a saucepan over low heat, stirring continually. Be careful not to scorch or burn the chocolate.

Transfer to a mixing bowl and add the sugar. Stir to mix and then beat in the eggs one at a time until the batter is smooth. Gently fold in the flour and then mix in the salt, vanilla, and crème de menthe. Sprinkle the berries with a little extra flour—this will help keep them from sinking to the bottom of the cake. Fold the blackberries into the batter.

Pour into the prepared baking dish and place in the oven. Bake for about 25 minutes, or until the cake has risen slightly and is barely cooked in the centre. Transfer to a cooling rack and allow to sit for at least 15 minutes. Cut into wedges and serve. The cake should be fairly moist in the centre.

Sauce

¼ cup (60 mL) butter

1 cup (250 mL) brown sugar

1 cup (250 mL) whipping cream

Cake

1 cup (250 mL) dried blueberries (or
  2 cups [500 mL] frozen berries)

zest and juice of 1 orange

2 cups (500 mL) all-purpose flour

1 tsp (5 mL) baking powder

¾ cup (175 mL) sugar

¼ tsp (1 mL) salt

⅓ cup (75 mL) butter

3 eggs

1 tsp (5 mL) vanilla extract

SERVES 4–6

STICKY TOFFEE BLUEBERRY PUDDING

This is a rich dish for winter nights or the celebration of gathering of family and friends. The cake is rich and dense and backed with dark blueberry flavours. To be honest, the cake is really just an excuse to make the toffee sauce. Try matching this dish with a glass of sweet sherry or a nice blackberry port.

Preheat the oven to 325°F (160°C).

To make the sauce, heat a saucepan over medium and add the butter, brown sugar, and whipping cream. Bring to a boil and stir to mix well. Remove from the heat and reserve until needed.

In a food processor, add the dried blueberries, orange zest, and orange juice. Pulse until a smooth paste is formed. Set aside until needed.

In a small bowl, combine the flour, baking powder, sugar, and salt. In a mixer, add the butter and beat until smooth. Add the eggs one at a time and beat until fully incorporated. Scrape down the sides of the bowl as needed. Add the vanilla and beat until the mixture is light and fluffy. Add the puréed blueberries and beat until smooth. Gently fold in the flour in batches until just mixed.

Butter and flour a springform pan (or Bundt pan or individual custard cups). Pour in the batter. Place on a roasting tray and place in the oven. Pour boiling water 1–2 inches (2.5–5 cm) deep in the tray. Cook for about 30–40 minutes for individual puddings, or 1 hour or more for the cake. Insert a toothpick into the cake to test; the toothpick should come out clean when cooked.

Serve warm (or reheat in a warm oven). Place on a serving plate, reheat the sauce, and spoon a little on top of the cake. Serve immediately.

3 Tbsp (45 mL) butter, melted
3 cups (750 mL) plums, pitted and quartered
½ cup (125 mL) packed brown sugar
¼ cup (60 mL) candied ginger, minced
½ cup (125 mL) butter, softened
¾ cup (175 mL) granulated sugar
2 eggs
2 tsp (10 mL) pure vanilla extract
1½ cups (375 mL) all-purpose flour
2 tsp (10 mL) baking powder
¼ tsp (1 mL) salt
⅛ tsp (0.5 mL) nutmeg
1 cup (250 mL) sour cream (or plain yogurt)

SERVES 6–8

WILD PLUM AND CANDIED GINGER CAKE

This cake is a master recipe for many variations. You can add blackberries, blueberries, or salal berries in place of the plums and achieve excellent results. This cake is flipped over once cooled so that the fruit forms a topping for the cake. The dessert is best the day it is made, although it will freeze nicely for up to 1 month.

Preheat the oven to 350°F (180°C).

In an 8-inch (20 cm) square glass (or non-stick) dish, mix the melted butter, plums, brown sugar, and ginger. Stir well to mix and spread evenly over the bottom of the dish.

In a stand mixer (or using a hand-held mixer), cream together softened butter and sugar until fluffy. Beat in the eggs, one at a time, mixing well after each addition. Add the vanilla. In a bowl, stir together the flour, baking powder, salt, and nutmeg. Fold one-third of the flour mixture into the creamed mixture, then add one-third of the sour cream. Alternate adding the flour mixture and the sour cream until all of the ingredients are just mixed.

Spread the batter over the plums. Bake in the oven for 45–50 minutes, or until the top springs back when lightly pressed. Let cool on a rack for 15 minutes. Run a knife around the edge of the pan; invert the cake onto a serving plate. Serve warm or at room temperature.

Cake

2 cups (500 mL) all-purpose flour

2 Tbsp (30 mL) sugar

1 Tbsp (15 mL) baking powder

½ tsp (2 mL) salt

½ cup (125 mL) butter

1 egg, beaten

⅔ cup (150 mL) whipping cream

Topping

1 cup (250 mL) whipping cream

2 Tbsp (30 mL) maple syrup

2 cups (500 mL) mixed wild berries

SERVES 6–8

WILD BERRY SHORTCAKE

This cake brings me back to my time in England, where they serve shortcakes (or scones) with strawberry jam and clotted Devonshire cream (kind of a full fat sour cream). You can make this with a number of berries but my favourites are blackberries, blueberries, and strawberries.

Preheat the oven to 425°F (220°C).

In a bowl, combine the flour, sugar, baking powder, and salt. Cut in the butter until the mixture resembles coarse crumbs. In a small bowl, whisk together the egg and whipping cream; add all at once to the crumb mixture and stir just until moistened. Spread the batter into a greased 8-inch (20 cm) round baking pan, slightly building up around the edges. Bake in the oven for 15–18 minutes, or until golden brown. Remove from the pan and cool on a wire rack.

In a small bowl, whisk the whipping cream until it just begins to thicken. Add the maple syrup; whisk until stiff peaks form. Split the cake in half widthwise. Spoon half of the berries over the bottom layer. Top with a spoonful of whipped cream. Cover with the top cake layer. Top with the remaining berries and whipped cream. Cut into squares or wedges.

4 large eggs
½ cup (125 mL) extra-virgin olive oil
1½ cups (375 mL) sugar
1 tsp (5 mL) salt
zest and juice of 1 large lemon
½ cup (125 mL) whole milk
1 cup (250 mL) ground hazelnuts
1 cup (250 mL) all-purpose flour
1 Tbsp (15 mL) baking powder

SERVES 6–8

OLIVE OIL AND HAZELNUT CAKE

When I first tried this recipe, I was skeptical about the combination of olive oil and hazelnuts—it turned out to be an incredible marriage. I have repeated the success with local black walnuts. I like to think any use of local nuts is a victory over the squirrels!

Preheat the oven to 350°F (180°C).

Oil a springform pan and dust with flour. Set aside until needed.

Separate the eggs and place the whites in a mixing bowl. Whip the whites to stiff peaks, then transfer to a clean bowl and set aside until needed. In the mixing bowl, cream the olive oil and sugar together. Beat in the egg yolks, one at a time until light and fluffy. Add the salt, lemon zest, lemon juice, and milk. Beat until a smooth batter is formed. Add the ground hazelnuts, flour, and baking powder and mix until just combined. Using a whisk, fold in the egg whites until smooth.

Fold the batter into the prepared pan. Place in the oven and bake for 45 minutes to 1 hour. Test with a toothpick until it comes out clean (free of batter). The cake should be golden and pulled away from the sides. Cool on a rack for 15 minutes and turn out onto a serving plate. Serve warm or at room temperature.

RESOURCES

Mycological Societies

Alberta Mycological Society *wildmushrooms.ws*

Le Cercle des Mycologues de Montreal
  mycomontreal.qc.ca

Mycological Society of Toronto *myctor.org*

North American Mycological Association *namyco.org*

S. Vancouver Island Mycological Society *svims.ca*

Vancouver Mycological Society *vanmyco.com*

ID Resources

Edible Wild Food *ediblewildfood.com*

Foraging Resources *foraging.com*

Mushroom Expert *mushroomexpert.com*

Mykoweb *mykoweb.com*

Northern Bush Craft *northernbushcraft.com*

Wild Crafting *wildcrafting.net*

Selected Mushroom and Wild Food Suppliers

Mikuni Wild Harvest *mikuniwildharvest*

Misty Mountain Mushrooms *mistymt.com*

Ponderosa Mushrooms *ponderosa.com*

Untamed Feast *untamedfeast.com*

Recommended Mushroom Guide Books

All the Rain Promises and More, David Arora, Ten
  Speed Press, 1991

Common Mushrooms of the Pacific Northwest,
  J. Duane Sept, Calypso Publishing, 2006

*The Complete Mushroom Hunter: An Illustrated
  Guide to Finding, Harvesting, and Enjoying Wild
  Mushrooms*, Gary Lincoff, Quarry Books, 2010

Mushrooms and Other Fungi of North America, Roger
  Phillips, Firefly Books, 2010

Mushrooms Demystified, David Arora, Ten Speed
  Press, 1986

Mushrooms of the Pacific Northwest, Steve Trudel and
  Joe Ammirati, Timber Press Field Guide, 2009

Recommended Foraging Guides and Cooking Books

Backyard Foraging, Ellen Zachos, Storey Publishing, 2013

*The Deerholme Mushroom Book: From Foraging to
  Feasting*, Bill Jones, TouchWood Editions, 2013

The Edible Seashore, Rick M. Harbo, Hancock House
  Publishers, 2005

Edible Wild Plants, John Kallas, Gibbs Smith, 2010

Food Plants of Coastal First Peoples, Nancy J. Turner,
  UBC Press, 1995

Food Plants of Interior First Nations, Nancy J. Turner,
  UBC Press, 1997

The Joy of Foraging, Gary Lincoff, Quarry Books, 2012

Nature's Garden, Samuel Thayer, Foragers Harvest
  Press, 2010

Northwestern Wild Berries, J.E. Underhill, Hancock
  House Publishers, 1980

*Pacific Feast: A Cook's Guide to West Coast Foraging
  and Cuisine*, Jennifer Hahn, Skipstone, 2010

Pacific Seaweeds, Louis Druehl, Harbour Publishing, 2000

Preserving Wild Food, Matthew Weingarten and Raquel
  Pelzel, Storey Publishing, 2012

*The Savoury Mushroom: Cooking with Wild and
  Cultivated Mushrooms*, Bill Jones, Raincoast Books,
  2000

Seashore of British Columbia, Ian Sheldon, Lone Pine
  Publishing, 1998

Self Sufficiency Foraging, David Squire, Skyhorse
  Publishing, 2011

Shells and Shellfish of the Pacific Northwest, Rick M.
  Harbo, Harbour Publishing, 1997

Stalking the Wild Asparagus, Euell Gibbons, Allan C.
  Hood & Company, 1962

The Wild Table: Seasonal Foraged Foods and Recipes,
  Connie Green and Sarah Scott, Viking Studio, 2010

Author Contact

Bill Jones

Deerholme Farm

deerholme.com

bill@deerholme.com

INDEX

ACKNOWLEDGMENTS

My heartfelt gratitude goes out to the great team at TouchWood Editions. They are dedicated to producing great books and their passion for the details shines through. Thanks to Ruth Linka, Pete Kohut, and Emily Shorthouse for their contributions on my behalf. I would like to particularly thank Cailey Cavallin for her helpful suggestions and editing of the manuscript. Her ideas greatly added to the logic and readability of the book.

On the home front, I would like to thank my wife, Lynn, for being an awesome gardener and lover of all plants and animals. Even pruning is painful to her, so we evolved our property into an expanding world of edible landscape, cottage flower garden, and managed forest. It's a never-ending project and we wouldn't have it any other way. My constant foraging companion is my lovable border collie, Oliver. He has become a big part of the farm and is always ready to go for a walk or protect me from squirrels as I forage (I don't dare tell him this is not completely necessary—he needs the job).

I would also like to thank the chef and farmer community of Vancouver Island, and the Cowichan Valley in particular. They have become my friends and partners in much of the food we create here at Deerholme Farm. The chefs in particular are generous with their time and they make our community-building efforts successful and fun. We even share foraging resources and intel. It is refreshing to be in a group of like-minded individuals who appreciate the environment and the community as much as they do.

We really are lucky to be living in a society where food is abundant and fresh. It is something we should not take for granted and we all need to support and encourage the local food community. We also need to protect the resources from overharvesting and habitat destruction. The farmers, fishermen, and food producers who feed us are a critical and underappreciated part of the food system. Without the people who make and forage our food, the world would be a much bleaker and hungrier place. Supporting local food is also important for the economy, the health of the community, and your own personal health. With wild foods, you ultimately have a choice to invest in education and forage for free or support those who can help bring the harvest to your table. Either way you will find yourself richer for the experience.

On a gentler note, to quote my dear friend, the late Urban Peasant, James Barber, "the secret to great cooking is to find amazing local ingredients and not screw them up." Wise words from my mentor and great friend, and words to really cook by.